TEACHER'S PET PUBLICATIONS

PUZZLE PACK
for
The Great Gilly Hopkins

based on the book by
Katherine Paterson

Written by
William T. Collins

© 2005 Teacher's Pet Publications
All Rights Reserved

The materials in this packet are copyrighted
by Teacher's Pet Publications, Inc.

These pages may be duplicated by the purchaser
for use in the purchaser's own classroom.

Copying any of these materials and distributing them
for any other purpose is a violation of the copyright laws.

© 2005 Teacher's Pet Publications, Inc.
www.tpet.com

INTRODUCTION
If you already own the LitPlan for this title, this Puzzle Pack will refresh your Unit Resource Materials and Vocabulary Resource Materials sections plus give you additional materials you can substitute into the tests. If you do not already have a complete LitPlan, these pages will give you some supplemental materials to use with your own plan. There are two main groups of materials: one set for unit words (such as characters' names, symbols, places, etc.) and one set for vocabulary words associated with the book.

WORD LIST
There is a word list for both the unit words and the vocabulary words. These lists show you which words are being used in the materials and the clues or definitions being used for those words. You may want to give students a word list with clues/definitions to help them, or you may want students to only have a word list (without clues/definitions) if you want them to work a little harder. Both are available for duplication. The word lists can also be your "calling key" for the bingo games.

FILL IN THE BLANK AND MATCHING
There are 4 each of the fill in the blank and matching worksheets for both the unit and vocabulary words. These pages can be used either as extra worksheets for students or as objective parts of a unit test. They can be done individually if students need extra help or as a whole class activity to review the material covered.

MAGIC SQUARES
The magic squares not only reinforce the material covered but also work on reasoning and math skills. Many teachers have told us that their students really enjoy doing these!

WORD SEARCH PUZZLES
The word search words go in all directions, as indicated on your answer keys. Two of the word search puzzles have the clues listed rather than the words. This makes the puzzle a little more difficult, but it reinforces the material better. Two word search puzzles have words only for students who find the clue puzzles too difficult.

CROSSWORD PUZZLES
Both unit and vocabulary word sections have 4 crossword puzzles.

BINGO CARDS
There are 32 individual bingo cards for the unit words and 32 individual bingo cards for the vocabulary words. You can use your word list as a "call list," calling the words at random and marking them off of your list as you go, or you could use the flash cards by cutting them apart and drawing the words at random from a hat (or box or whatever). To make a better review, you might ask for the definition and spelling of each word as you call it out–or you could call out the definitions and have students tell you the words they need to look for on the puzzle.

JUGGLE LETTERS
The vocabulary juggle letter game is intended to help students learn the spellings of the words. One sheet has the definitions listed on it as an extra help for students who need it or to reinforce the definitions if you choose to do so.

FLASH CARDS
We've included a set of vocabulary flash cards you can duplicate, cut, and fold for your students. Some teachers make a few sets for general use by the class; others make a set for each student. Some teachers duplicate them for each student and have the students cut & fold their own. You can cut out just the words and put them in a hat, have each student pick out one word and write the definition and a sentence for that word. Students then swap words and papers, with the next student adding a sentence of his own under the last one. You can have students swap as many times as you like. Each time the student will read the sentences written prior to his own and then add a sentence. You can cut out the words and definitions separately and play "I Have; Who Has?" Each student in the room draws a word and definition. The first student says, "I have (the name of the word). Who has the definition?" The student with the definition reads it then says, "I have (the name of the vocabulary word she has). Who has the definition?" The round continues until all words and definitions have been given.

Great Gilly Hopkins Word List

No.	Word	Clue/Definition
1.	APTITUDE	National _____; test Gilly scored highest on
2.	BLACK	Gilly was afraid to touch someone this color
3.	BOOKS	Hundreds of them fill Mr. Randolph's house
4.	BUBBLE	____ gum; Gilly stuck it under left-hand car door handle
5.	CALIFORNIA	Postmark on Courtney's postcard
6.	CHADWELL	Courtney's brother who died in Vietnam
7.	CLASSROOM	Harris-6 is Gilly's new ___
8.	CLOUDS	____ of Glory; imaginary horse Gilly writes about to W.E.
9.	DANDELION	Meanest flower that blows
10.	DEFEND	W.E. learns to do this from Gilly
11.	DULLES	Airport where Courtney arrives
12.	EARNEST	William ____: bespectacled younger foster brother
13.	ELLIS	Miss____; caseworker for Gilly
14.	EVANS	Mr. ____ insists on no fighting at school
15.	FLU	Virus all except Gilly caught around Thanksgiving
16.	FRANCISCO	Ticket to San ____ cost $136.60
17.	GOOD	____Book; The Holy Bible
18.	GRUESOME	____Gilly; nickname main character gives herself
19.	HARRIS	Miss ____; Gilly writes poem for her
20.	HELP	What everyone was offering Gilly
21.	HOLLYWOOD	____ Garden: where the Nevin's live
22.	HOPKINS	Galadriel____; eleven year-old foster girl
23.	INSCRIPTION	For my beautiful Galadriel
24.	JACKSON	Town in Virginia where Nonnie lives
25.	NEVINS	Gilly's most recent foster parents
26.	NONNIE	Courtney's mother
27.	ORANGE	Reading group W.E. got promoted to
28.	PAPER	____airplane; 'It sure fly good.'
29.	PATERSON	Author
30.	POW	W.E.'s favorite word
31.	RANDOLPH	Mr. ____ eats meals at Maime Trotter's
32.	RECESS	Gilly takes basketball away here
33.	RELIGIOUS	____ fanatic; what Gilly thinks of Trotter at first
34.	RINSE	Nonnie's new hair coloring job
35.	RUTHERFORD	Courtney____ Hopkins; mother who abandons Gilly
36.	SESAME	____ Street; W.E.'s favorite TV program
37.	SIX	___ to one; odds in playground fight
38.	STOKES	Agnes ____ lives with her grandmother
39.	TEN	Number of dollars that fall out from behind encyclopedia
40.	THIRTEEN	Number of years since Nonnie had heard from Courtney
41.	THIRTY	Amount of money W.E. found for Gilly: ___-four
42.	THOMPSON	____ Park; location of foster home in Maryland
43.	THREE	Age when Gilly had seen her mother
44.	TOLKEIN	Author of books Miss Harris sends Gilly
45.	TROTTER	Maime____; hippopotamus of a woman
46.	WAY	Gilly bought a One-____ticket
47.	WORDSWORTH	Poet who wrote about the 'trailing clouds of glory'

Copyrighted

Great Gilly Hopkins Fill In The Blanks 1

_____ 1. Miss _____; Gilly writes poem for her

_____ 2. Courtney's brother who died in Vietnam

_____ 3. Amount of money W.E. found for Gilly: ____-four

_____ 4. Gilly bought a One-____ticket

_____ 5. W.E. learns to do this from Gilly

_____ 6. Town in Virginia where Nonnie lives

_____ 7. Postmark on Courtney's postcard

_____ 8. ____airplane; 'It sure fly good.'

_____ 9. Miss____; caseworker for Gilly

_____ 10. Courtney's mother

_____ 11. Ticket to San ____ cost $136.60

_____ 12. ____ Street; W.E.'s favorite TV program

_____ 13. Gilly's most recent foster parents

_____ 14. Age when Gilly had seen her mother

_____ 15. Agnes ____ lives with her grandmother

_____ 16. For my beautiful Galadriel

_____ 17. Courtney____ Hopkins; mother who abandons Gilly

_____ 18. Virus all except Gilly caught around Thanksgiving

_____ 19. Mr. ____ insists on no fighting at school

_____ 20. William ____: bespectacled younger foster brother

Great Gilly Hopkins Fill In The Blanks 1 Answer Key

HARRIS	1. Miss ____; Gilly writes poem for her
CHADWELL	2. Courtney's brother who died in Vietnam
THIRTY	3. Amount of money W.E. found for Gilly: ____-four
WAY	4. Gilly bought a One-____ ticket
DEFEND	5. W.E. learns to do this from Gilly
JACKSON	6. Town in Virginia where Nonnie lives
CALIFORNIA	7. Postmark on Courtney's postcard
PAPER	8. ____ airplane; 'It sure fly good.'
ELLIS	9. Miss ____; caseworker for Gilly
NONNIE	10. Courtney's mother
FRANCISCO	11. Ticket to San ____ cost $136.60
SESAME	12. ____ Street; W.E.'s favorite TV program
NEVINS	13. Gilly's most recent foster parents
THREE	14. Age when Gilly had seen her mother
STOKES	15. Agnes ____ lives with her grandmother
INSCRIPTION	16. For my beautiful Galadriel
RUTHERFORD	17. Courtney ____ Hopkins; mother who abandons Gilly
FLU	18. Virus all except Gilly caught around Thanksgiving
EVANS	19. Mr. ____ insists on no fighting at school
EARNEST	20. William ____: bespectacled younger foster brother

Great Gilly Hopkins Fill In The Blanks 2

_____ 1. ____Book; The Holy Bible

_____ 2. W.E.'s favorite word

_____ 3. Gilly was afraid to touch someone this color

_____ 4. Reading group W.E. got promoted to

_____ 5. Gilly takes basketball away here

_____ 6. Miss ____; Gilly writes poem for her

_____ 7. ____ Garden: where the Nevin's live

_____ 8. For my beautiful Galadriel

_____ 9. ____ gum; Gilly stuck it under left-hand car door handle

_____ 10. ____ Park; location of foster home in Maryland

_____ 11. William ____: bespectacled younger foster brother

_____ 12. Ticket to San ____ cost $136.60

_____ 13. ____ fanatic; what Gilly thinks of Trotter at first

_____ 14. Gilly bought a One-____ticket

_____ 15. Mr. ____ insists on no fighting at school

_____ 16. ____airplane; 'It sure fly good.'

_____ 17. Airport where Courtney arrives

_____ 18. Courtney____ Hopkins; mother who abandons Gilly

_____ 19. Hundreds of them fill Mr. Randolph's house

_____ 20. Author of books Miss Harris sends Gilly

Great Gilly Hopkins Fill In The Blanks 2 Answer Key

GOOD	1. ____ Book; The Holy Bible
POW	2. W.E.'s favorite word
BLACK	3. Gilly was afraid to touch someone this color
ORANGE	4. Reading group W.E. got promoted to
RECESS	5. Gilly takes basketball away here
HARRIS	6. Miss ____; Gilly writes poem for her
HOLLYWOOD	7. ____ Garden: where the Nevin's live
INSCRIPTION	8. For my beautiful Galadriel
BUBBLE	9. ____ gum; Gilly stuck it under left-hand car door handle
THOMPSON	10. ____ Park; location of foster home in Maryland
EARNEST	11. William ____: bespectacled younger foster brother
FRANCISCO	12. Ticket to San ____ cost $136.60
RELIGIOUS	13. ____ fanatic; what Gilly thinks of Trotter at first
WAY	14. Gilly bought a One-____ ticket
EVANS	15. Mr. ____ insists on no fighting at school
PAPER	16. ____ airplane; 'It sure fly good.'
DULLES	17. Airport where Courtney arrives
RUTHERFORD	18. Courtney ____ Hopkins; mother who abandons Gilly
BOOKS	19. Hundreds of them fill Mr. Randolph's house
TOLKEIN	20. Author of books Miss Harris sends Gilly

Great Gilly Hopkins Fill In The Blanks 3

1. ____Gilly; nickname main character gives herself
2. Author of books Miss Harris sends Gilly
3. ____ Garden: where the Nevin's live
4. Age when Gilly had seen her mother
5. Airport where Courtney arrives
6. Town in Virginia where Nonnie lives
7. ____ gum; Gilly stuck it under left-hand car door handle
8. Postmark on Courtney's postcard
9. Gilly takes basketball away here
10. Harris-6 is Gilly's new ___
11. Number of years since Nonnie had heard from Courtney
12. W.E.'s favorite word
13. Number of dollars that fall out from behind encyclopedia
14. Nonnie's new hair coloring job
15. Miss____; caseworker for Gilly
16. Ticket to San ____ cost $136.60
17. Courtney____ Hopkins; mother who abandons Gilly
18. Miss ____; Gilly writes poem for her
19. Virus all except Gilly caught around Thanksgiving
20. ____airplane; 'It sure fly good.'

Great Gilly Hopkins Fill In The Blanks 3 Answer Key

GRUESOME	1. ____Gilly; nickname main character gives herself
TOLKEIN	2. Author of books Miss Harris sends Gilly
HOLLYWOOD	3. ____ Garden: where the Nevin's live
THREE	4. Age when Gilly had seen her mother
DULLES	5. Airport where Courtney arrives
JACKSON	6. Town in Virginia where Nonnie lives
BUBBLE	7. ____ gum; Gilly stuck it under left-hand car door handle
CALIFORNIA	8. Postmark on Courtney's postcard
RECESS	9. Gilly takes basketball away here
CLASSROOM	10. Harris-6 is Gilly's new ___
THIRTEEN	11. Number of years since Nonnie had heard from Courtney
POW	12. W.E.'s favorite word
TEN	13. Number of dollars that fall out from behind encyclopedia
RINSE	14. Nonnie's new hair coloring job
ELLIS	15. Miss____; caseworker for Gilly
FRANCISCO	16. Ticket to San ____ cost $136.60
RUTHERFORD	17. Courtney____ Hopkins; mother who abandons Gilly
HARRIS	18. Miss ____; Gilly writes poem for her
FLU	19. Virus all except Gilly caught around Thanksgiving
PAPER	20. ____airplane; 'It sure fly good.'

Great Gilly Hopkins Fill In The Blanks 4

1. ____ gum; Gilly stuck it under left-hand car door handle
2. ____ fanatic; what Gilly thinks of Trotter at first
3. Number of dollars that fall out from behind encyclopedia
4. Age when Gilly had seen her mother
5. Reading group W.E. got promoted to
6. Number of years since Nonnie had heard from Courtney
7. Gilly was afraid to touch someone this color
8. Author
9. Galadriel____; eleven year-old foster girl
10. Ticket to San ____ cost $136.60
11. Courtney's brother who died in Vietnam
12. Miss____; caseworker for Gilly
13. Gilly's most recent foster parents
14. Mr. ____ insists on no fighting at school
15. Mr. ____ eats meals at Maime Trotter's
16. Author of books Miss Harris sends Gilly
17. Courtney____ Hopkins; mother who abandons Gilly
18. Courtney's mother
19. Airport where Courtney arrives
20. Agnes ____ lives with her grandmother

Great Gilly Hopkins Fill In The Blanks 4 Answer Key

BUBBLE	1. ____ gum; Gilly stuck it under left-hand car door handle
RELIGIOUS	2. ____ fanatic; what Gilly thinks of Trotter at first
TEN	3. Number of dollars that fall out from behind encyclopedia
THREE	4. Age when Gilly had seen her mother
ORANGE	5. Reading group W.E. got promoted to
THIRTEEN	6. Number of years since Nonnie had heard from Courtney
BLACK	7. Gilly was afraid to touch someone this color
PATERSON	8. Author
HOPKINS	9. Galadriel____; eleven year-old foster girl
FRANCISCO	10. Ticket to San ____ cost $136.60
CHADWELL	11. Courtney's brother who died in Vietnam
ELLIS	12. Miss____; caseworker for Gilly
NEVINS	13. Gilly's most recent foster parents
EVANS	14. Mr. ____ insists on no fighting at school
RANDOLPH	15. Mr. ____ eats meals at Maime Trotter's
TOLKEIN	16. Author of books Miss Harris sends Gilly
RUTHERFORD	17. Courtney____ Hopkins; mother who abandons Gilly
NONNIE	18. Courtney's mother
DULLES	19. Airport where Courtney arrives
STOKES	20. Agnes ____ lives with her grandmother

Great Gilly Hopkins Matching 1

___ 1. JACKSON   A. ____airplane; 'It sure fly good.'
___ 2. NEVINS   B. What everyone was offering Gilly
___ 3. FRANCISCO   C. ____ Park; location of foster home in Maryland
___ 4. RECESS   D. Galadriel____; eleven year-old foster girl
___ 5. DANDELION   E. Gilly takes basketball away here
___ 6. ELLIS   F. Gilly was afraid to touch someone this color
___ 7. SESAME   G. National_____; test Gilly scored highest on
___ 8. HOPKINS   H. Miss____; caseworker for Gilly
___ 9. HELP   I. ___ to one; odds in playground fight
___ 10. CLOUDS   J. Gilly bought a One-____ticket
___ 11. TEN   K. Maime____; hippopotamus of a woman
___ 12. THIRTY   L. Author of books Miss Harris sends Gilly
___ 13. SIX   M. Amount of money W.E. found for Gilly: ___-four
___ 14. GRUESOME   N. ____ of Glory; imaginary horse Gilly writes about to W.E.
___ 15. PATERSON   O. Meanest flower that blows
___ 16. RINSE   P. Town in Virginia where Nonnie lives
___ 17. TROTTER   Q. ____Gilly; nickname main character gives herself
___ 18. STOKES   R. Gilly's most recent foster parents
___ 19. POW   S. Number of dollars that fall out from behind encyclopedia
___ 20. PAPER   T. ____ Street; W.E.'s favorite TV program
___ 21. TOLKEIN   U. Nonnie's new hair coloring job
___ 22. BLACK   V. Ticket to San ____ cost $136.60
___ 23. WAY   W. Author
___ 24. APTITUDE   X. W.E.'s favorite word
___ 25. THOMPSON   Y. Agnes ____ lives with her grandmother

Great Gilly Hopkins Matching 1 Answer Key

P - 1. JACKSON   A. ____airplane; 'It sure fly good.'
R - 2. NEVINS   B. What everyone was offering Gilly
V - 3. FRANCISCO   C. ____ Park; location of foster home in Maryland
E - 4. RECESS   D. Galadriel____; eleven year-old foster girl
O - 5. DANDELION   E. Gilly takes basketball away here
H - 6. ELLIS   F. Gilly was afraid to touch someone this color
T - 7. SESAME   G. National____; test Gilly scored highest on
D - 8. HOPKINS   H. Miss____; caseworker for Gilly
B - 9. HELP   I. ____ to one; odds in playground fight
N -10. CLOUDS   J. Gilly bought a One-____ticket
S -11. TEN   K. Maime____; hippopotamus of a woman
M -12. THIRTY   L. Author of books Miss Harris sends Gilly
I -13. SIX   M. Amount of money W.E. found for Gilly: ____-four
Q -14. GRUESOME   N. ____ of Glory; imaginary horse Gilly writes about to W.E.
W -15. PATERSON   O. Meanest flower that blows
U -16. RINSE   P. Town in Virginia where Nonnie lives
K -17. TROTTER   Q. ____Gilly; nickname main character gives herself
Y -18. STOKES   R. Gilly's most recent foster parents
X -19. POW   S. Number of dollars that fall out from behind encyclopedia
A -20. PAPER   T. ____ Street; W.E.'s favorite TV program
L -21. TOLKEIN   U. Nonnie's new hair coloring job
F -22. BLACK   V. Ticket to San ____ cost $136.60
J -23. WAY   W. Author
G -24. APTITUDE   X. W.E.'s favorite word
C -25. THOMPSON   Y. Agnes ____ lives with her grandmother

Great Gilly Hopkins Matching 2

___ 1. GRUESOME   A. Author
___ 2. SESAME   B. Airport where Courtney arrives
___ 3. CHADWELL   C. Postmark on Courtney's postcard
___ 4. THOMPSON   D. Number of years since Nonnie had heard from Courtney
___ 5. HOLLYWOOD   E. Gilly's most recent foster parents
___ 6. PATERSON   F. Amount of money W.E. found for Gilly: ___-four
___ 7. THIRTY   G. Town in Virginia where Nonnie lives
___ 8. THIRTEEN   H. For my beautiful Galadriel
___ 9. PAPER   I. ____ Street; W.E.'s favorite TV program
___10. NEVINS   J. ____airplane; 'It sure fly good.'
___11. CLASSROOM   K. Ticket to San ____ cost $136.60
___12. CLOUDS   L. Maime____; hippopotamus of a woman
___13. FLU   M. Gilly takes basketball away here
___14. RECESS   N. Virus all except Gilly caught around Thanksgiving
___15. WORDSWORTH   O. ____ gum; Gilly stuck it under left-hand car door handle
___16. BUBBLE   P. Mr. ____ insists on no fighting at school
___17. EVANS   Q. ____ of Glory; imaginary horse Gilly writes about to W.E.
___18. DANDELION   R. ____Gilly; nickname main character gives herself
___19. TEN   S. Harris-6 is Gilly's new ____
___20. CALIFORNIA   T. ____ Park; location of foster home in Maryland
___21. INSCRIPTION   U. ____ Garden: where the Nevin's live
___22. FRANCISCO   V. Courtney's brother who died in Vietnam
___23. JACKSON   W. Poet who wrote about the 'trailing clouds of glory'
___24. TROTTER   X. Meanest flower that blows
___25. DULLES   Y. Number of dollars that fall out from behind encyclopedia

Great Gilly Hopkins Matching 2 Answer Key

R - 1. GRUESOME   A. Author
I - 2. SESAME   B. Airport where Courtney arrives
V - 3. CHADWELL   C. Postmark on Courtney's postcard
T - 4. THOMPSON   D. Number of years since Nonnie had heard from Courtney
U - 5. HOLLYWOOD   E. Gilly's most recent foster parents
A - 6. PATERSON   F. Amount of money W.E. found for Gilly: ____-four
F - 7. THIRTY   G. Town in Virginia where Nonnie lives
D - 8. THIRTEEN   H. For my beautiful Galadriel
J - 9. PAPER   I. ____ Street; W.E.'s favorite TV program
E - 10. NEVINS   J. ____ airplane; 'It sure fly good.'
S - 11. CLASSROOM   K. Ticket to San ____ cost $136.60
Q - 12. CLOUDS   L. Maime____; hippopotamus of a woman
N - 13. FLU   M. Gilly takes basketball away here
M - 14. RECESS   N. Virus all except Gilly caught around Thanksgiving
W - 15. WORDSWORTH   O. ____ gum; Gilly stuck it under left-hand car door handle
O - 16. BUBBLE   P. Mr. ____ insists on no fighting at school
P - 17. EVANS   Q. ____ of Glory; imaginary horse Gilly writes about to W.E.
X - 18. DANDELION   R. ____ Gilly; nickname main character gives herself
Y - 19. TEN   S. Harris-6 is Gilly's new ____
C - 20. CALIFORNIA   T. ____ Park; location of foster home in Maryland
H - 21. INSCRIPTION   U. ____ Garden: where the Nevin's live
K - 22. FRANCISCO   V. Courtney's brother who died in Vietnam
G - 23. JACKSON   W. Poet who wrote about the 'trailing clouds of glory'
L - 24. TROTTER   X. Meanest flower that blows
B - 25. DULLES   Y. Number of dollars that fall out from behind encyclopedia

Great Gilly Hopkins Matching 3

___ 1. STOKES   A. ____ airplane; 'It sure fly good.'
___ 2. DEFEND   B. Author of books Miss Harris sends Gilly
___ 3. TROTTER   C. Amount of money W.E. found for Gilly: ___-four
___ 4. THIRTY   D. ____ of Glory; imaginary horse Gilly writes about to W.E.
___ 5. RELIGIOUS   E. Agnes ____ lives with her grandmother
___ 6. RECESS   F. ___ to one; odds in playground fight
___ 7. HOPKINS   G. ____ fanatic; what Gilly thinks of Trotter at first
___ 8. SESAME   H. Galadriel____; eleven year-old foster girl
___ 9. POW   I. Airport where Courtney arrives
___10. THIRTEEN   J. Nonnie's new hair coloring job
___11. CLOUDS   K. Mr. ____ insists on no fighting at school
___12. HARRIS   L. National____; test Gilly scored highest on
___13. BOOKS   M. Gilly takes basketball away here
___14. THREE   N. Miss ____; Gilly writes poem for her
___15. DULLES   O. W.E.'s favorite word
___16. CLASSROOM   P. Age when Gilly had seen her mother
___17. HOLLYWOOD   Q. ____ Garden: where the Nevin's live
___18. APTITUDE   R. Hundreds of them fill Mr. Randolph's house
___19. TOLKEIN   S. W.E. learns to do this from Gilly
___20. SIX   T. For my beautiful Galadriel
___21. EVANS   U. ____ Book; The Holy Bible
___22. PAPER   V. Harris-6 is Gilly's new ____
___23. RINSE   W. Maime____; hippopotamus of a woman
___24. GOOD   X. Number of years since Nonnie had heard from Courtney
___25. INSCRIPTION   Y. ____ Street; W.E.'s favorite TV program

Great Gilly Hopkins Matching 3 Answer Key

E - 1. STOKES	A.	____airplane; 'It sure fly good.'
S - 2. DEFEND	B.	Author of books Miss Harris sends Gilly
W - 3. TROTTER	C.	Amount of money W.E. found for Gilly: ___-four
C - 4. THIRTY	D.	____ of Glory; imaginary horse Gilly writes about to W.E.
G - 5. RELIGIOUS	E.	Agnes ____ lives with her grandmother
M - 6. RECESS	F.	___ to one; odds in playground fight
H - 7. HOPKINS	G.	____ fanatic; what Gilly thinks of Trotter at first
Y - 8. SESAME	H.	Galadriel____; eleven year-old foster girl
O - 9. POW	I.	Airport where Courtney arrives
X - 10. THIRTEEN	J.	Nonnie's new hair coloring job
D - 11. CLOUDS	K.	Mr. ____ insists on no fighting at school
N - 12. HARRIS	L.	National____; test Gilly scored highest on
R - 13. BOOKS	M.	Gilly takes basketball away here
P - 14. THREE	N.	Miss ____; Gilly writes poem for her
I - 15. DULLES	O.	W.E.'s favorite word
V - 16. CLASSROOM	P.	Age when Gilly had seen her mother
Q - 17. HOLLYWOOD	Q.	____ Garden: where the Nevin's live
L - 18. APTITUDE	R.	Hundreds of them fill Mr. Randolph's house
B - 19. TOLKEIN	S.	W.E. learns to do this from Gilly
F - 20. SIX	T.	For my beautiful Galadriel
K - 21. EVANS	U.	____Book; The Holy Bible
A - 22. PAPER	V.	Harris-6 is Gilly's new ___
J - 23. RINSE	W.	Maime____; hippopotamus of a woman
U - 24. GOOD	X.	Number of years since Nonnie had heard from Courtney
T - 25. INSCRIPTION	Y.	____ Street; W.E.'s favorite TV program

Great Gilly Hopkins Matching 4

___ 1. RUTHERFORD　　A. ____ Street; W.E.'s favorite TV program
___ 2. ELLIS　　B. Ticket to San ____ cost $136.60
___ 3. WAY　　C. Gilly bought a One-____ticket
___ 4. PAPER　　D. Gilly was afraid to touch someone this color
___ 5. INSCRIPTION　　E. Postmark on Courtney's postcard
___ 6. CALIFORNIA　　F. Courtney____ Hopkins; mother who abandons Gilly
___ 7. BLACK　　G. Author of books Miss Harris sends Gilly
___ 8. HARRIS　　H. Mr. ____ eats meals at Maime Trotter's
___ 9. RANDOLPH　　I. W.E.'s favorite word
___10. NEVINS　　J. W.E. learns to do this from Gilly
___11. JACKSON　　K. Gilly takes basketball away here
___12. THOMPSON　　L. Number of years since Nonnie had heard from Courtney
___13. GOOD　　M. For my beautiful Galadriel
___14. THIRTEEN　　N. Author
___15. TOLKEIN　　O. ____Book; The Holy Bible
___16. HELP　　P. Miss____; caseworker for Gilly
___17. RECESS　　Q. ____Gilly; nickname main character gives herself
___18. WORDSWORTH　　R. Miss ____; Gilly writes poem for her
___19. DEFEND　　S. Gilly's most recent foster parents
___20. GRUESOME　　T. ____ Park; location of foster home in Maryland
___21. FRANCISCO　　U. Town in Virginia where Nonnie lives
___22. TROTTER　　V. ____airplane; 'It sure fly good.'
___23. POW　　W. Poet who wrote about the 'trailing clouds of glory'
___24. PATERSON　　X. Maime____; hippopotamus of a woman
___25. SESAME　　Y. What everyone was offering Gilly

Great Gilly Hopkins Matching 4 Answer Key

F - 1. RUTHERFORD	A. ____ Street; W.E.'s favorite TV program
P - 2. ELLIS	B. Ticket to San ____ cost $136.60
C - 3. WAY	C. Gilly bought a One-____ ticket
V - 4. PAPER	D. Gilly was afraid to touch someone this color
M - 5. INSCRIPTION	E. Postmark on Courtney's postcard
E - 6. CALIFORNIA	F. Courtney ____ Hopkins; mother who abandons Gilly
D - 7. BLACK	G. Author of books Miss Harris sends Gilly
R - 8. HARRIS	H. Mr. ____ eats meals at Maime Trotter's
H - 9. RANDOLPH	I. W.E.'s favorite word
S - 10. NEVINS	J. W.E. learns to do this from Gilly
U - 11. JACKSON	K. Gilly takes basketball away here
T - 12. THOMPSON	L. Number of years since Nonnie had heard from Courtney
O - 13. GOOD	M. For my beautiful Galadriel
L - 14. THIRTEEN	N. Author
G - 15. TOLKEIN	O. ____ Book; The Holy Bible
Y - 16. HELP	P. Miss ____; caseworker for Gilly
K - 17. RECESS	Q. ____ Gilly; nickname main character gives herself
W - 18. WORDSWORTH	R. Miss ____; Gilly writes poem for her
J - 19. DEFEND	S. Gilly's most recent foster parents
Q - 20. GRUESOME	T. ____ Park; location of foster home in Maryland
B - 21. FRANCISCO	U. Town in Virginia where Nonnie lives
X - 22. TROTTER	V. ____ airplane; 'It sure fly good.'
I - 23. POW	W. Poet who wrote about the 'trailing clouds of glory'
N - 24. PATERSON	X. Maime ____; hippopotamus of a woman
A - 25. SESAME	Y. What everyone was offering Gilly

Great Gilly Hopkins Magic Squares 1

Match the definition with the vocabulary word. Put your answers in the magic squares below. When your answers are correct, all columns and rows will add to the same number.

A. DULLES
B. NEVINS
C. FRANCISCO
D. RECESS
E. POW
F. RINSE
G. BLACK
H. TROTTER
I. THIRTY
J. BUBBLE
K. DANDELION
L. CALIFORNIA
M. CLASSROOM
N. HARRIS
O. FLU
P. GRUESOME

1. Maime ____; hippopotamus of a woman
2. Harris-6 is Gilly's new ____
3. Gilly's most recent foster parents
4. Meanest flower that blows
5. ____ gum; Gilly stuck it under left-hand car door handle
6. Ticket to San ____ cost $136.60
7. ____ Gilly; nickname main character gives herself
8. W.E.'s favorite word
9. Virus all except Gilly caught around Thanksgiving
10. Nonnie's new hair coloring job
11. Amount of money W.E. found for Gilly: ____-four
12. Gilly takes basketball away here
13. Airport where Courtney arrives
14. Postmark on Courtney's postcard
15. Gilly was afraid to touch someone this color
16. Miss ____; Gilly writes poem for her

A=	B=	C=	D=
E=	F=	G=	H=
I=	J=	K=	L=
M=	N=	O=	P=

21
Copyrighted

Great Gilly Hopkins Magic Squares 1 Answer Key

Match the definition with the vocabulary word. Put your answers in the magic squares below. When your answers are correct, all columns and rows will add to the same number.

A. DULLES
B. NEVINS
C. FRANCISCO
D. RECESS
E. POW
F. RINSE
G. BLACK
H. TROTTER
I. THIRTY
J. BUBBLE
K. DANDELION
L. CALIFORNIA
M. CLASSROOM
N. HARRIS
O. FLU
P. GRUESOME

1. Maime____; hippopotamus of a woman
2. Harris-6 is Gilly's new ___
3. Gilly's most recent foster parents
4. Meanest flower that blows
5. ____ gum; Gilly stuck it under left-hand car door handle
6. Ticket to San ____ cost $136.60
7. ____Gilly; nickname main character gives herself
8. W.E.'s favorite word
9. Virus all except Gilly caught around Thanksgiving
10. Nonnie's new hair coloring job
11. Amount of money W.E. found for Gilly: ___-four
12. Gilly takes basketball away here
13. Airport where Courtney arrives
14. Postmark on Courtney's postcard
15. Gilly was afraid to touch someone this color
16. Miss ____; Gilly writes poem for her

A=13	B=3	C=6	D=12
E=8	F=10	G=15	H=1
I=11	J=5	K=4	L=14
M=2	N=16	O=9	P=7

Great Gilly Hopkins Magic Squares 2

Match the definition with the vocabulary word. Put your answers in the magic squares below. When your answers are correct, all columns and rows will add to the same number.

A. THOMPSON　　E. GRUESOME　　I. CHADWELL　　M. WAY
B. TEN　　　　　　F. ORANGE　　　J. RELIGIOUS　　N. BUBBLE
C. NEVINS　　　　G. GOOD　　　　K. THIRTEEN　　O. JACKSON
D. THIRTY　　　　H. HARRIS　　　L. STOKES　　　P. RANDOLPH

1. ____ gum; Gilly stuck it under left-hand car door handle
2. ____ Book; The Holy Bible
3. Agnes ____ lives with her grandmother
4. ____ Park; location of foster home in Maryland
5. Number of years since Nonnie had heard from Courtney
6. Number of dollars that fall out from behind encyclopedia
7. Gilly bought a One-____ ticket
8. Miss ____; Gilly writes poem for her
9. ____ Gilly; nickname main character gives herself
10. Mr. ____ eats meals at Maime Trotter's
11. Gilly's most recent foster parents
12. ____ fanatic; what Gilly thinks of Trotter at first
13. Amount of money W.E. found for Gilly: ____-four
14. Courtney's brother who died in Vietnam
15. Reading group W.E. got promoted to
16. Town in Virginia where Nonnie lives

A=	B=	C=	D=
E=	F=	G=	H=
I=	J=	K=	L=
M=	N=	O=	P=

Great Gilly Hopkins Magic Squares 2 Answer Key

Match the definition with the vocabulary word. Put your answers in the magic squares below. When your answers are correct, all columns and rows will add to the same number.

A. THOMPSON   E. GRUESOME   I. CHADWELL   M. WAY
B. TEN   F. ORANGE   J. RELIGIOUS N. BUBBLE
C. NEVINS   G. GOOD   K. THIRTEEN   O. JACKSON
D. THIRTY   H. HARRIS   L. STOKES   P. RANDOLPH

1. ____ gum; Gilly stuck it under left-hand car door handle
2. ____ Book; The Holy Bible
3. Agnes ____ lives with her grandmother
4. ____ Park; location of foster home in Maryland
5. Number of years since Nonnie had heard from Courtney
6. Number of dollars that fall out from behind encyclopedia
7. Gilly bought a One-____ ticket
8. Miss ____; Gilly writes poem for her
9. ____ Gilly; nickname main character gives herself
10. Mr. ____ eats meals at Maime Trotter's
11. Gilly's most recent foster parents
12. ____ fanatic; what Gilly thinks of Trotter at first
13. Amount of money W.E. found for Gilly: ____-four
14. Courtney's brother who died in Vietnam
15. Reading group W.E. got promoted to
16. Town in Virginia where Nonnie lives

A=4	B=6	C=11	D=13
E=9	F=15	G=2	H=8
I=14	J=12	K=5	L=3
M=7	N=1	O=16	P=10

Great Gilly Hopkins Magic Squares 3

Match the definition with the vocabulary word. Put your answers in the magic squares below. When your answers are correct, all columns and rows will add to the same number.

A. CALIFORNIA	E. DULLES	I. CLASSROOM	M. INSCRIPTION
B. APTITUDE	F. EVANS	J. HOPKINS	N. RUTHERFORD
C. THIRTEEN	G. BOOKS	K. EARNEST	O. TOLKEIN
D. BLACK	H. PAPER	L. ELLIS	P. JACKSON

1. For my beautiful Galadriel
2. Mr. ____ insists on no fighting at school
3. ____ airplane; 'It sure fly good.'
4. Author of books Miss Harris sends Gilly
5. Miss ____; caseworker for Gilly
6. Number of years since Nonnie had heard from Courtney
7. Postmark on Courtney's postcard
8. Galadriel ____; eleven year-old foster girl
9. William ____: bespectacled younger foster brother
10. Gilly was afraid to touch someone this color
11. National ____; test Gilly scored highest on
12. Harris-6 is Gilly's new ___
13. Courtney ____ Hopkins; mother who abandons Gilly
14. Airport where Courtney arrives
15. Hundreds of them fill Mr. Randolph's house
16. Town in Virginia where Nonnie lives

A=	B=	C=	D=
E=	F=	G=	H=
I=	J=	K=	L=
M=	N=	O=	P=

Great Gilly Hopkins Magic Squares 3 Answer Key

Match the definition with the vocabulary word. Put your answers in the magic squares below. When your answers are correct, all columns and rows will add to the same number.

A. CALIFORNIA
B. APTITUDE
C. THIRTEEN
D. BLACK
E. DULLES
F. EVANS
G. BOOKS
H. PAPER
I. CLASSROOM
J. HOPKINS
K. EARNEST
L. ELLIS
M. INSCRIPTION
N. RUTHERFORD
O. TOLKEIN
P. JACKSON

1. For my beautiful Galadriel
2. Mr. ____ insists on no fighting at school
3. ____ airplane; 'It sure fly good.'
4. Author of books Miss Harris sends Gilly
5. Miss ____; caseworker for Gilly
6. Number of years since Nonnie had heard from Courtney
7. Postmark on Courtney's postcard
8. Galadriel ____; eleven year-old foster girl
9. William ____: bespectacled younger foster brother
10. Gilly was afraid to touch someone this color
11. National ____; test Gilly scored highest on
12. Harris-6 is Gilly's new ___
13. Courtney ____ Hopkins; mother who abandons Gilly
14. Airport where Courtney arrives
15. Hundreds of them fill Mr. Randolph's house
16. Town in Virginia where Nonnie lives

A=7	B=11	C=6	D=10
E=14	F=2	G=15	H=3
I=12	J=8	K=9	L=5
M=1	N=13	O=4	P=16

Great Gilly Hopkins Magic Squares 4

Match the definition with the vocabulary word. Put your answers in the magic squares below. When your answers are correct, all columns and rows will add to the same number.

A. HOLLYWOOD E. ORANGE   I. TOLKEIN   M. THREE
B. WORDSWORTH F. CALIFORNIA   J. CHADWELL   N. BOOKS
C. SESAME   G. HARRIS   K. DANDELION   O. BUBBLE
D. GRUESOME   H. RELIGIOUS   L. EVANS   P. THIRTY

1. ____ gum; Gilly stuck it under left-hand car door handle
2. ____ Gilly; nickname main character gives herself
3. Courtney's brother who died in Vietnam
4. Reading group W.E. got promoted to
5. Author of books Miss Harris sends Gilly
6. Postmark on Courtney's postcard
7. Amount of money W.E. found for Gilly: ____-four
8. ____ Street; W.E.'s favorite TV program
9. ____ fanatic; what Gilly thinks of Trotter at first
10. Meanest flower that blows
11. ____ Garden: where the Nevin's live
12. Hundreds of them fill Mr. Randolph's house
13. Poet who wrote about the 'trailing clouds of glory'
14. Age when Gilly had seen her mother
15. Miss ____; Gilly writes poem for her
16. Mr. ____ insists on no fighting at school

A=	B=	C=	D=
E=	F=	G=	H=
I=	J=	K=	L=
M=	N=	O=	P=

27
Copyrighted

Great Gilly Hopkins Magic Squares 4 Answer Key

Match the definition with the vocabulary word. Put your answers in the magic squares below. When your answers are correct, all columns and rows will add to the same number.

A. HOLLYWOOD
B. WORDSWORTH
C. SESAME
D. GRUESOME
E. ORANGE
F. CALIFORNIA
G. HARRIS
H. RELIGIOUS
I. TOLKEIN
J. CHADWELL
K. DANDELION
L. EVANS
M. THREE
N. BOOKS
O. BUBBLE
P. THIRTY

1. ____ gum; Gilly stuck it under left-hand car door handle
2. ____Gilly; nickname main character gives herself
3. Courtney's brother who died in Vietnam
4. Reading group W.E. got promoted to
5. Author of books Miss Harris sends Gilly
6. Postmark on Courtney's postcard
7. Amount of money W.E. found for Gilly: ___-four
8. ____ Street; W.E.'s favorite TV program
9. ____ fanatic; what Gilly thinks of Trotter at first
10. Meanest flower that blows
11. ____ Garden: where the Nevin's live
12. Hundreds of them fill Mr. Randolph's house
13. Poet who wrote about the 'trailing clouds of glory'
14. Age when Gilly had seen her mother
15. Miss ____; Gilly writes poem for her
16. Mr. ____ insists on no fighting at school

A=11	B=13	C=8	D=2
E=4	F=6	G=15	H=9
I=5	J=3	K=10	L=16
M=14	N=12	O=1	P=7

Great Gilly Hopkins Word Search 1

```
R R F T C B T T W O R D S W O R T H E C
Z E D E H H H G A R W I U L C T B S G M
M G C N R I A P Y V X T O E F D N A N V
Y O K E R K R D T G N N I M J I W P A R
V O E T S E R T W P I V G O R D R T R L
T D E Z M S L Y Y E A Z I S V N S I O F
C E Q A M J T L K L L T L E R E B T T N
N L S K R W H L I B N L E U N F F U R P
Q E O E P Y O R R S E P R R Z E N D O S
S V P U K T M A L T V Y A G S D X E T F
N A Z B D T P N J P I E L K K O C H T B
P C E X Y S S D D A N D E L I O N Y E F
H O L L Y W O O D L S Z K Y C W Y H R R
T N B V B H N L J H B C E Z F B A A X N
M S B V K G Y P J A A P V T N R N E R Z
K T U C G W Z H K L C Q A K R C I P P X
G O B N D R T R B B J K N I I N B U S W
F K Q D Q R Y D U L L E S S N P L E H T
V E R U T H E R F O R D C O M F F H T D
M S N I K P O H P O W O N K N B O O K S
```

Age when Gilly had seen her mother (5)
Agnes ____ lives with her grandmother (6)
Airport where Courtney arrives (6)
Amount of money W.E. found for Gilly: ___-four (6)
Author (8)
Author of books Miss Harris sends Gilly (7)
Courtney's brother who died in Vietnam (8)
Courtney's mother (6)
Courtney____ Hopkins; mother who abandons Gilly (10)
Galadriel____; eleven year-old foster girl (7)
Gilly bought a One-____ticket (3)
Gilly takes basketball away here (6)
Gilly was afraid to touch someone this color (5)
Gilly's most recent foster parents (6)
Hundreds of them fill Mr. Randolph's house (5)
Maime____; hippopotamus of a woman (7)
Meanest flower that blows (9)
Miss ____; Gilly writes poem for her (6)
Miss____; caseworker for Gilly (5)
Mr. ____ eats meals at Maime Trotter's (8)
Mr. ____ insists on no fighting at school (5)
National_____; test Gilly scored highest on (8)
Nonnie's new hair coloring job (5)
Number of dollars that fall out from behind encyclopedia (3)
Number of years since Nonnie had heard from Courtney (8)

Poet who wrote about the 'trailing clouds of glory' (10)
Reading group W.E. got promoted to (6)
Ticket to San ____ cost $136.60 (9)
Town in Virginia where Nonnie lives (7)
Virus all except Gilly caught around Thanksgiving (3)
W.E. learns to do this from Gilly (6)
W.E.'s favorite word (3)
What everyone was offering Gilly (4)
William ____: bespectacled younger foster brother (7)
___ to one; odds in playground fight (3)
____ Garden: where the Nevin's live (9)
____ Park; location of foster home in Maryland (8)
____ Street; W.E.'s favorite TV program (6)
____ fanatic; what Gilly thinks of Trotter at first (9)
____ gum; Gilly stuck it under left-hand car door handle (6)
____ of Glory; imaginary horse Gilly writes about to W.E. (6)
____Book; The Holy Bible (4)
____Gilly; nickname main character gives herself (8)
____airplane; 'It sure fly good.' (5)

Great Gilly Hopkins Word Search 1 Answer Key

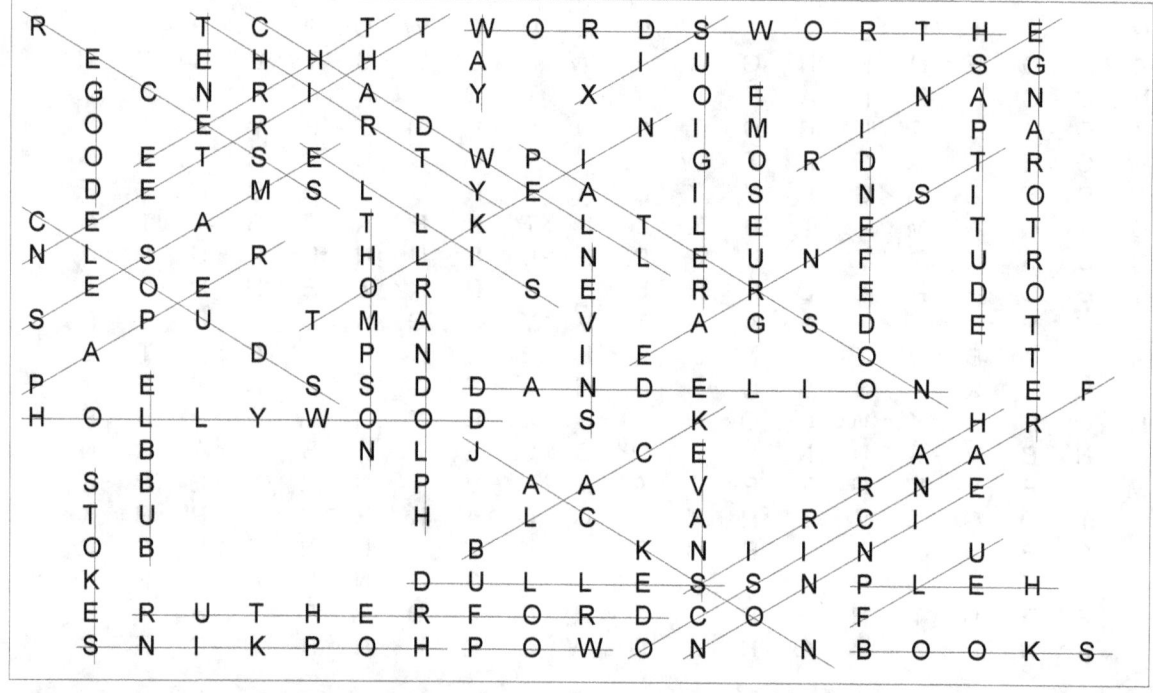

Age when Gilly had seen her mother (5)
Agnes ____ lives with her grandmother (6)
Airport where Courtney arrives (6)
Amount of money W.E. found for Gilly: ____-four (6)
Author (8)
Author of books Miss Harris sends Gilly (7)
Courtney's brother who died in Vietnam (8)
Courtney's mother (6)
Courtney____ Hopkins; mother who abandons Gilly (10)
Galadriel____; eleven year-old foster girl (7)
Gilly bought a One-____ticket (3)
Gilly takes basketball away here (6)
Gilly was afraid to touch someone this color (5)
Gilly's most recent foster parents (6)
Hundreds of them fill Mr. Randolph's house (5)
Maime____; hippopotamus of a woman (7)
Meanest flower that blows (9)
Miss ____; Gilly writes poem for her (6)
Miss____; caseworker for Gilly (5)
Mr. ____ eats meals at Maime Trotter's (8)
Mr. ____ insists on no fighting at school (5)
National____; test Gilly scored highest on (8)
Nonnie's new hair coloring job (5)
Number of dollars that fall out from behind encyclopedia (3)
Number of years since Nonnie had heard from Courtney (8)

Poet who wrote about the 'trailing clouds of glory' (10)
Reading group W.E. got promoted to (6)
Ticket to San ____ cost $136.60 (9)
Town in Virginia where Nonnie lives (7)
Virus all except Gilly caught around Thanksgiving (3)
W.E. learns to do this from Gilly (6)
W.E.'s favorite word (3)
What everyone was offering Gilly (4)
William ____: bespectacled younger foster brother (7)
____ to one; odds in playground fight (3)
____ Garden: where the Nevin's live (9)
____ Park; location of foster home in Maryland (8)
____ Street; W.E.'s favorite TV program (6)
____ fanatic; what Gilly thinks of Trotter at first (9)
____ gum; Gilly stuck it under left-hand car door handle (6)
____ of Glory; imaginary horse Gilly writes about to W.E. (6)
____Book; The Holy Bible (4)
____Gilly; nickname main character gives herself (8)
____airplane; 'It sure fly good.' (5)

Great Gilly Hopkins Word Search 2

```
R J Q W L E G Q N O S K C A J R T F C F
W E D G P J L Q E Z T D K T T A H S L V
N A C K R V T L V H M F R O Z N I T O V
H V Y E H A R R I S S E L L U D R O U N
R F J P S B O R N S P K D G R O T K D M
L Y D P B S T Y S A E L E O M L Y E S V
R M L H K E T D P I U L F W O P T S K Q
K E T C E S E S N T X R E O O H P E S D
H G A N V A R Z W J E B N R R N K D N Z
L L F D M M B E O H B O D D S O C A A V
B S Z Z K E M C T T S O J S S N A N V B
E F Q T M O S U D P H K F W A N L D E G
L A F X S I R F M Z P S H O L I I E L S
T P R E C S U O I G I L E R C E F L B N
O B U N Y C H A D W E L L T S E O I B J
L R A J E T H O P K I N S H E Q R O U F
G R A D E S N I R P A T E R S O N N B T
F Z O N F T T J G M H Z H N F R I T R S
W O N C G H E D U T I T P A V Y A D B H
G W Y W L E I N S C R I P T I O N G M K
```

Age when Gilly had seen her mother (5)
Agnes ____ lives with her grandmother (6)
Airport where Courtney arrives (6)
Amount of money W.E. found for Gilly: ____-four (6)
Author (8)
Author of books Miss Harris sends Gilly (7)
Courtney's brother who died in Vietnam (8)
Courtney's mother (6)
Courtney____ Hopkins; mother who abandons Gilly (10)
For my beautiful Galadriel (11)
Galadriel____; eleven year-old foster girl (7)
Gilly bought a One-____ticket (3)
Gilly takes basketball away here (6)
Gilly was afraid to touch someone this color (5)
Gilly's most recent foster parents (6)
Harris-6 is Gilly's new ____ (9)
Hundreds of them fill Mr. Randolph's house (5)
Maime____; hippopotamus of a woman (7)
Meanest flower that blows (9)
Miss ____; Gilly writes poem for her (6)
Miss____; caseworker for Gilly (5)
Mr. ____ eats meals at Maime Trotter's (8)
Mr. ____ insists on no fighting at school (5)
National____; test Gilly scored highest on (8)
Nonnie's new hair coloring job (5)
Number of dollars that fall out from behind encyclopedia (3)
Number of years since Nonnie had heard from Courtney (8)
Poet who wrote about the 'trailing clouds of glory' (10)
Postmark on Courtney's postcard (10)
Reading group W.E. got promoted to (6)
Ticket to San ____ cost $136.60 (9)
Town in Virginia where Nonnie lives (7)
Virus all except Gilly caught around Thanksgiving (3)
W.E. learns to do this from Gilly (6)
W.E.'s favorite word (3)
What everyone was offering Gilly (4)
William ____: bespectacled younger foster brother (7)
___ to one; odds in playground fight (3)
____ Park; location of foster home in Maryland (8)
____ Street; W.E.'s favorite TV program (6)
____ fanatic; what Gilly thinks of Trotter at first (9)
____ gum; Gilly stuck it under left-hand car door handle (6)
____ of Glory; imaginary horse Gilly writes about to W.E. (6)
____Book; The Holy Bible (4)
____Gilly; nickname main character gives herself (8)
____airplane; 'It sure fly good.' (5)

Great Gilly Hopkins Word Search 2 Answer Key

Age when Gilly had seen her mother (5)
Agnes ____ lives with her grandmother (6)
Airport where Courtney arrives (6)
Amount of money W.E. found for Gilly: ____-four (6)
Author (8)
Author of books Miss Harris sends Gilly (7)
Courtney's brother who died in Vietnam (8)
Courtney's mother (6)
Courtney____ Hopkins; mother who abandons Gilly (10)
For my beautiful Galadriel (11)
Galadriel____; eleven year-old foster girl (7)
Gilly bought a One-____ticket (3)
Gilly takes basketball away here (6)
Gilly was afraid to touch someone this color (5)
Gilly's most recent foster parents (6)
Harris-6 is Gilly's new ____ (9)
Hundreds of them fill Mr. Randolph's house (5)
Maime____; hippopotamus of a woman (7)
Meanest flower that blows (9)
Miss ____; Gilly writes poem for her (6)
Miss____; caseworker for Gilly (5)
Mr. ____ eats meals at Maime Trotter's (8)
Mr. ____ insists on no fighting at school (5)
National____; test Gilly scored highest on (8)
Nonnie's new hair coloring job (5)
Number of dollars that fall out from behind encyclopedia (3)
Number of years since Nonnie had heard from Courtney (8)
Poet who wrote about the 'trailing clouds of glory' (10)
Postmark on Courtney's postcard (10)
Reading group W.E. got promoted to (6)
Ticket to San ____ cost $136.60 (9)
Town in Virginia where Nonnie lives (7)
Virus all except Gilly caught around Thanksgiving (3)
W.E. learns to do this from Gilly (6)
W.E.'s favorite word (3)
What everyone was offering Gilly (4)
William ____: bespectacled younger foster brother (7)
____ to one; odds in playground fight (3)
____ Park; location of foster home in Maryland (8)
____ Street; W.E.'s favorite TV program (6)
____ fanatic; what Gilly thinks of Trotter at first (9)
____ gum; Gilly stuck it under left-hand car door handle (6)
____ of Glory; imaginary horse Gilly writes about to W.E. (6)
____Book; The Holy Bible (4)
____Gilly; nickname main character gives herself (8)
____airplane; 'It sure fly good.' (5)

Great Gilly Hopkins Word Search 3

```
C H A D W E L L F R A N C I S C O E N W
Q G L Y P Y Y Y D B B H V G W S I B O J
D O Q T A K F X T H O M P S O N S R G Z
E O L R T R E L I G I O U S N H D G R S
F D H A E D W D C K S E K O T S F R U T
E A Y N R T V R A L J X N S W I S P E P
N P L D S N N O L F O Q F O P L D A S S
D T Y O O Z X F I G M U R F V L A P O M
C I W L N W K R F O J T D X D E N E M W
R T N P H P N E O R H N L S U N D R E N
W U B H T O G H R A N I L M L E E F N S
R D L H S H B T N N Q E Y H L E L S G D
X E A K B G I U I G D K O V E T I H E W
J J C T S E N R A E C L A S S R O O M H
F A K E L H E L T K L O Z N R I N P A T
J F T B S T X T T Y D T I A H H X K S F
P N B X T S Y F W L T V H V E T Y I E M
W U P O W C G O N G E F C E L R I N S E
B A R D V X O E F N F L H H P K Z S H R
N T Y S C D T Y B Z T U T H R E E H G N
```

APTITUDE	DULLES	HOLLYWOOD	RECESS	THOMPSON
BLACK	EARNEST	HOPKINS	RELIGIOUS	THREE
BOOKS	ELLIS	JACKSON	RINSE	TOLKEIN
BUBBLE	EVANS	NEVINS	RUTHERFORD	TROTTER
CALIFORNIA	FLU	NONNIE	SESAME	WAY
CHADWELL	FRANCISCO	ORANGE	SIX	WORDSWORTH
CLASSROOM	GOOD	PAPER	STOKES	
CLOUDS	GRUESOME	PATERSON	TEN	
DANDELION	HARRIS	POW	THIRTEEN	
DEFEND	HELP	RANDOLPH	THIRTY	

Great Gilly Hopkins Word Search 3 Answer Key

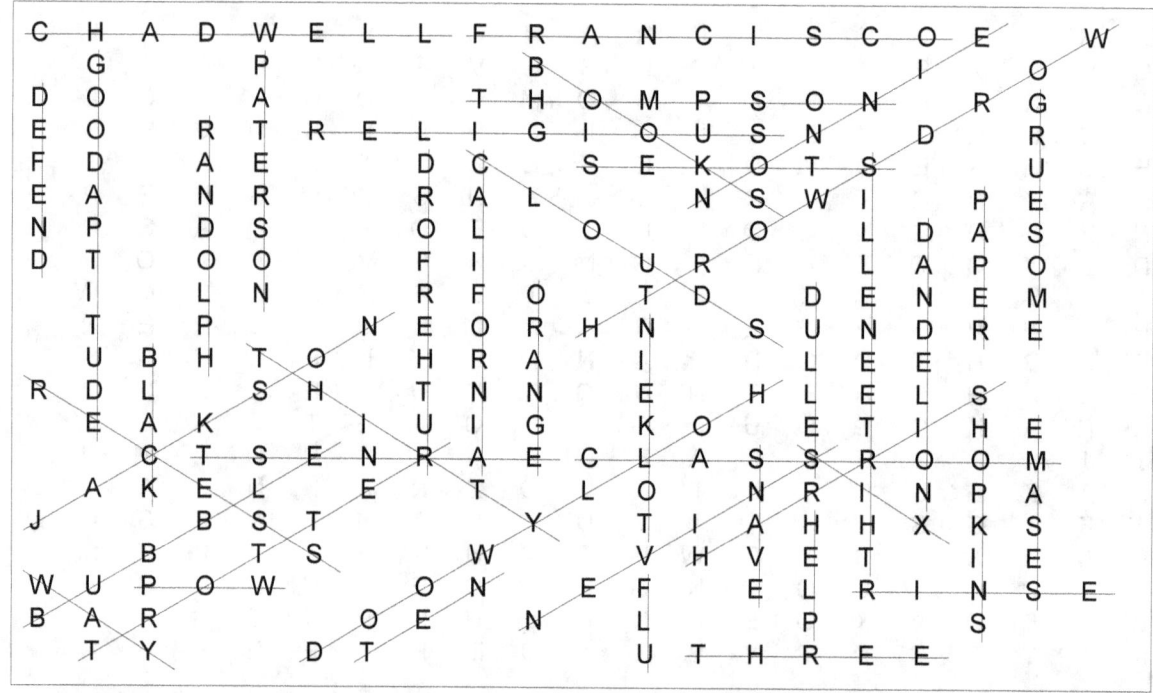

APTITUDE	DULLES	HOLLYWOOD	RECESS	THOMPSON
BLACK	EARNEST	HOPKINS	RELIGIOUS	THREE
BOOKS	ELLIS	JACKSON	RINSE	TOLKEIN
BUBBLE	EVANS	NEVINS	RUTHERFORD	TROTTER
CALIFORNIA	FLU	NONNIE	SESAME	WAY
CHADWELL	FRANCISCO	ORANGE	SIX	WORDSWORTH
CLASSROOM	GOOD	PAPER	STOKES	
CLOUDS	GRUESOME	PATERSON	TEN	
DANDELION	HARRIS	POW	THIRTEEN	
DEFEND	HELP	RANDOLPH	THIRTY	

Great Gilly Hopkins Word Search 4

```
G H O L L Y W O O D N E V I N S C J S B
W R M Z M V B B N N R R W C O P L J E L
J E U S K V X E V O A F F H S Z A H S Z
Z D S E J S F H D N N K S A P T S F A T
C U C S S E G W A N D T Y D M W S S M C
T T R X D O C M N I O D P W O T R P E Z
X I Z P H S M W D E L H U E H H O A R D
S T J L R K G E E Q P D W L T R O T E J
J P D M D O H X L T H O T L L E M E P H
C A L I F O R N I A Y A W T S E N R A E
F F C Y P B B G O Q T T Y H L R S S P E
L R J K H Q T S N N F C T B Q J I O G L
U A I H S T H I R T Y R B L A C K N S Z
J N G A N O J L X X O U D T L C A E S R
S C O R A H N L I W B L S B S R W E E E
S I O R V E L E S T V D K E O N N T C E
D S D I E L F D R Z U V K E E Q T R E D
J C T S X P R W Y O G O X T I O Y I R K
X O L M S O K N L M T K H F R N P H N Q
X C R H W T C C M S J M K T V F C T B C
```

APTITUDE	DEFEND	HARRIS	PATERSON	THIRTEEN
BLACK	DULLES	HELP	POW	THIRTY
BOOKS	EARNEST	HOLLYWOOD	RANDOLPH	THOMPSON
BUBBLE	ELLIS	HOPKINS	RECESS	THREE
CALIFORNIA	EVANS	JACKSON	RINSE	TOLKEIN
CHADWELL	FLU	NEVINS	SESAME	TROTTER
CLASSROOM	FRANCISCO	NONNIE	SIX	WAY
CLOUDS	GOOD	ORANGE	STOKES	WORDSWORTH
DANDELION	GRUESOME	PAPER	TEN	

Great Gilly Hopkins Word Search 4 Answer Key

APTITUDE	DEFEND	HARRIS	PATERSON	THIRTEEN
BLACK	DULLES	HELP	POW	THIRTY
BOOKS	EARNEST	HOLLYWOOD	RANDOLPH	THOMPSON
BUBBLE	ELLIS	HOPKINS	RECESS	THREE
CALIFORNIA	EVANS	JACKSON	RINSE	TOLKEIN
CHADWELL	FLU	NEVINS	SESAME	TROTTER
CLASSROOM	FRANCISCO	NONNIE	SIX	WAY
CLOUDS	GOOD	ORANGE	STOKES	WORDSWORTH
DANDELION	GRUESOME	PAPER	TEN	

Great Gilly Hopkins Crossword 1

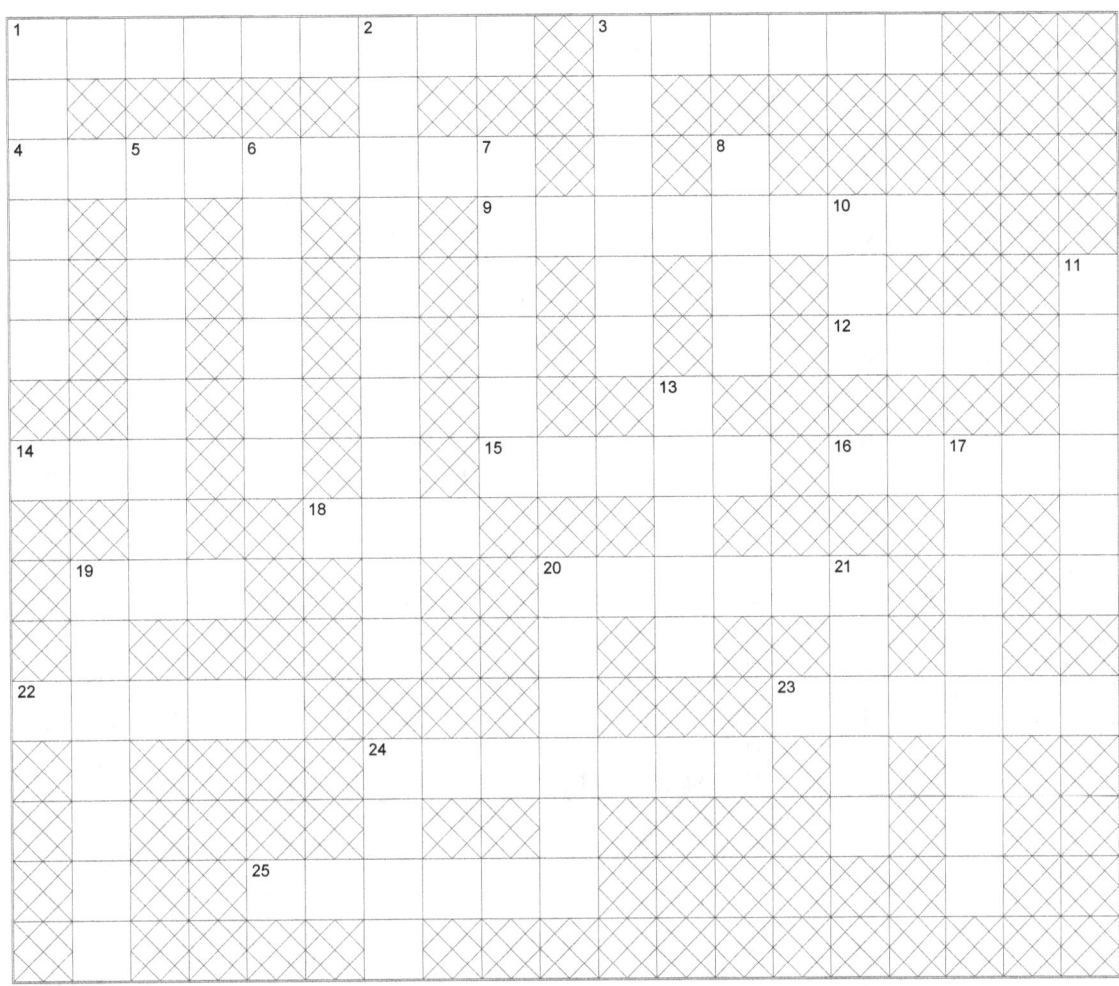

Across
1. Meanest flower that blows
3. Gilly's most recent foster parents
4. Ticket to San ____ cost $136.60
9. Mr. ____ eats meals at Maime Trotter's
12. Gilly bought a One-____ticket
14. Virus all except Gilly caught around Thanksgiving
15. Miss____; caseworker for Gilly
16. ____airplane; 'It sure fly good.'
18. ___ to one; odds in playground fight
19. Number of dollars that fall out from behind encyclopedia
20. ____ Street; W.E.'s favorite TV program
22. Hundreds of them fill Mr. Randolph's house
23. Miss ____; Gilly writes poem for her
24. Galadriel____; eleven year-old foster girl
25. Airport where Courtney arrives

Down
1. W.E. learns to do this from Gilly
2. For my beautiful Galadriel
3. Courtney's mother
5. National____; test Gilly scored highest on
6. ____ of Glory; imaginary horse Gilly writes about to W.E.
7. Reading group W.E. got promoted to
8. ____Book; The Holy Bible
10. W.E.'s favorite word
11. Amount of money W.E. found for Gilly: ____-four
13. Nonnie's new hair coloring job
17. Author
19. Maime____; hippopotamus of a woman
20. Agnes ____ lives with her grandmother
21. Mr. ____ insists on no fighting at school
24. What everyone was offering Gilly

Great Gilly Hopkins Crossword 1 Answer Key

	1 D	A	N	D	E	2 L	I	O	N		3 N	E	V	I	N	S		
	E					N					O							
	4 F	5 R	A	6 N	C	I	S	7 C	O		N		8 G					
	E	P		L				9 C	R	A	N	D	O	L	P	H		
	N	T		O				R			I		O					11 T
	D	I		U				I			E		D			12 W	A	Y
		T		U				P			G		13 R					H
	14 F	L	U		S		T			15 E	L	L	I	S		16 P	A	17 P	E	R
			D				18 S	I	X				N					A	T
		19 T	E	N			O				20 S	E	S	A	M	21 E		T	Y
		R					N				T		E			V		E	
	22 B	O	O	K	S						O				23 H	A	R	R	I	S
		T				24 H	O	P	K	I	N	S			N			S	
		T				E					E				S			O	
		E			25 D	U	L	L	E	S								N	
		R				P													

Across
1. Meanest flower that blows
3. Gilly's most recent foster parents
4. Ticket to San ____ cost $136.60
9. Mr. ____ eats meals at Maime Trotter's
12. Gilly bought a One-____ ticket
14. Virus all except Gilly caught around Thanksgiving
15. Miss____; caseworker for Gilly
16. ____airplane; 'It sure fly good.'
18. ___ to one; odds in playground fight
19. Number of dollars that fall out from behind encyclopedia
20. ____ Street; W.E.'s favorite TV program
22. Hundreds of them fill Mr. Randolph's house
23. Miss ____; Gilly writes poem for her
24. Galadriel____; eleven year-old foster girl
25. Airport where Courtney arrives

Down
1. W.E. learns to do this from Gilly
2. For my beautiful Galadriel
3. Courtney's mother
5. National____; test Gilly scored highest on
6. ____ of Glory; imaginary horse Gilly writes about to W.E.
7. Reading group W.E. got promoted to
8. ____Book; The Holy Bible
10. W.E.'s favorite word
11. Amount of money W.E. found for Gilly: ___-four
13. Nonnie's new hair coloring job
17. Author
19. Maime____; hippopotamus of a woman
20. Agnes ____ lives with her grandmother
21. Mr. ____ insists on no fighting at school
24. What everyone was offering Gilly

Great Gilly Hopkins Crossword 2

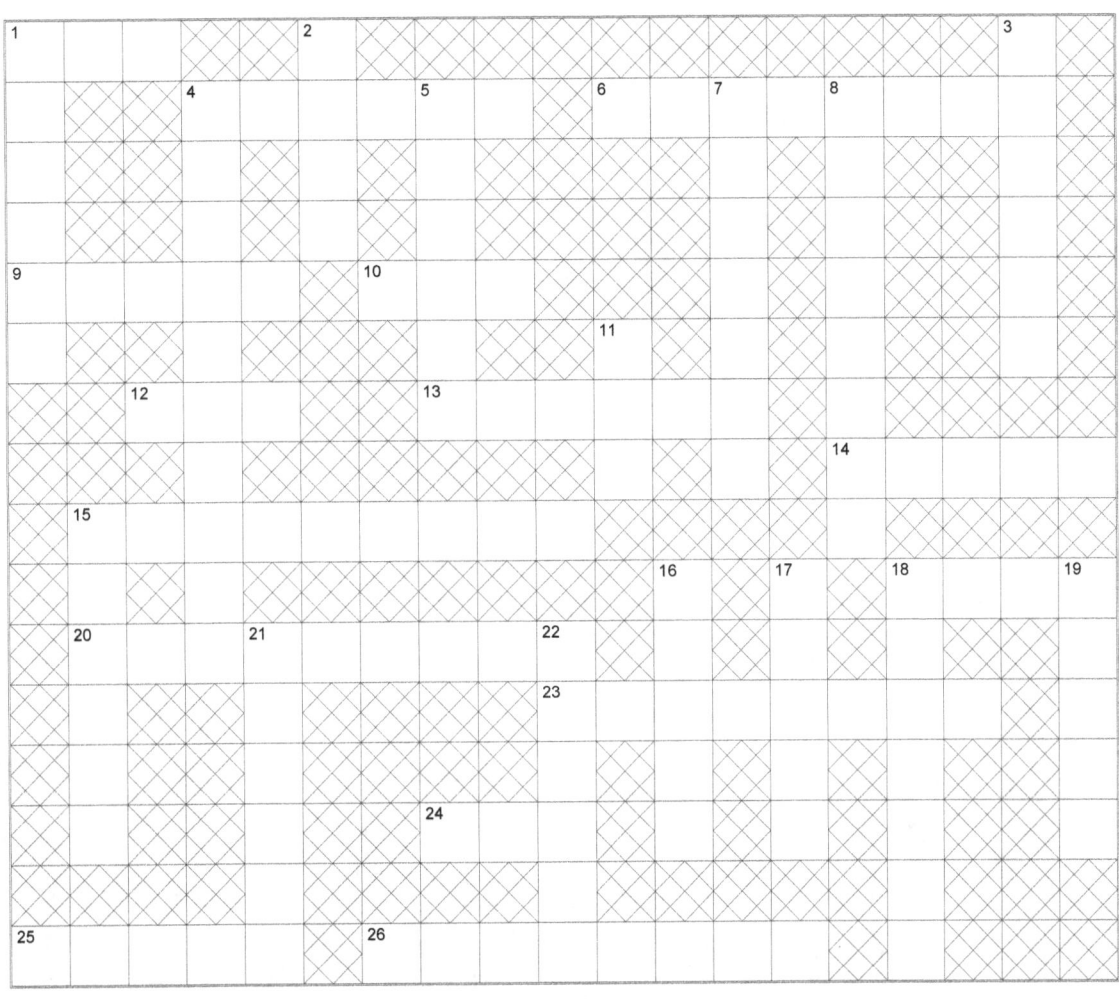

Across
1. ___ to one; odds in playground fight
4. ___ of Glory; imaginary horse Gilly writes about to W.E.
6. National___; test Gilly scored highest on
9. Miss___; caseworker for Gilly
10. Virus all except Gilly caught around Thanksgiving
12. W.E.'s favorite word
13. ___ Street; W.E.'s favorite TV program
14. Mr. ___ insists on no fighting at school
15. Meanest flower that blows
18. What everyone was offering Gilly
20. Ticket to San ___ cost $136.60
23. Mr. ___ eats meals at Maime Trotter's
24. Number of dollars that fall out from behind encyclopedia
25. Age when Gilly had seen her mother
26. Author

Down
1. Agnes ___ lives with her grandmother
2. ___ Book; The Holy Bible
3. Gilly's most recent foster parents
4. Postmark on Courtney's postcard
5. Airport where Courtney arrives
7. Maime___; hippopotamus of a woman
8. Number of years since Nonnie had heard from Courtney
11. Gilly bought a One-___ticket
15. W.E. learns to do this from Gilly
16. Nonnie's new hair coloring job
17. Hundreds of them fill Mr. Randolph's house
18. Galadriel___; eleven year-old foster girl
19. ___airplane; 'It sure fly good.'
21. Courtney's mother
22. Reading group W.E. got promoted to

Great Gilly Hopkins Crossword 2 Answer Key

Across
1. ___ to one; odds in playground fight
4. ____ of Glory; imaginary horse Gilly writes about to W.E.
6. National____; test Gilly scored highest on
9. Miss____; caseworker for Gilly
10. Virus all except Gilly caught around Thanksgiving
12. W.E.'s favorite word
13. ____ Street; W.E.'s favorite TV program
14. Mr. ____ insists on no fighting at school
15. Meanest flower that blows
18. What everyone was offering Gilly
20. Ticket to San ____ cost $136.60
23. Mr. ____ eats meals at Maime Trotter's
24. Number of dollars that fall out from behind encyclopedia
25. Age when Gilly had seen her mother
26. Author

Down
1. Agnes ____ lives with her grandmother
2. ____ Book; The Holy Bible
3. Gilly's most recent foster parents
4. Postmark on Courtney's postcard
5. Airport where Courtney arrives
7. Maime____; hippopotamus of a woman
8. Number of years since Nonnie had heard from Courtney
11. Gilly bought a One-____ ticket
15. W.E. learns to do this from Gilly
16. Nonnie's new hair coloring job
17. Hundreds of them fill Mr. Randolph's house
18. Galadriel____; eleven year-old foster girl
19. ____ airplane; 'It sure fly good.'
21. Courtney's mother
22. Reading group W.E. got promoted to

Great Gilly Hopkins Crossword 3

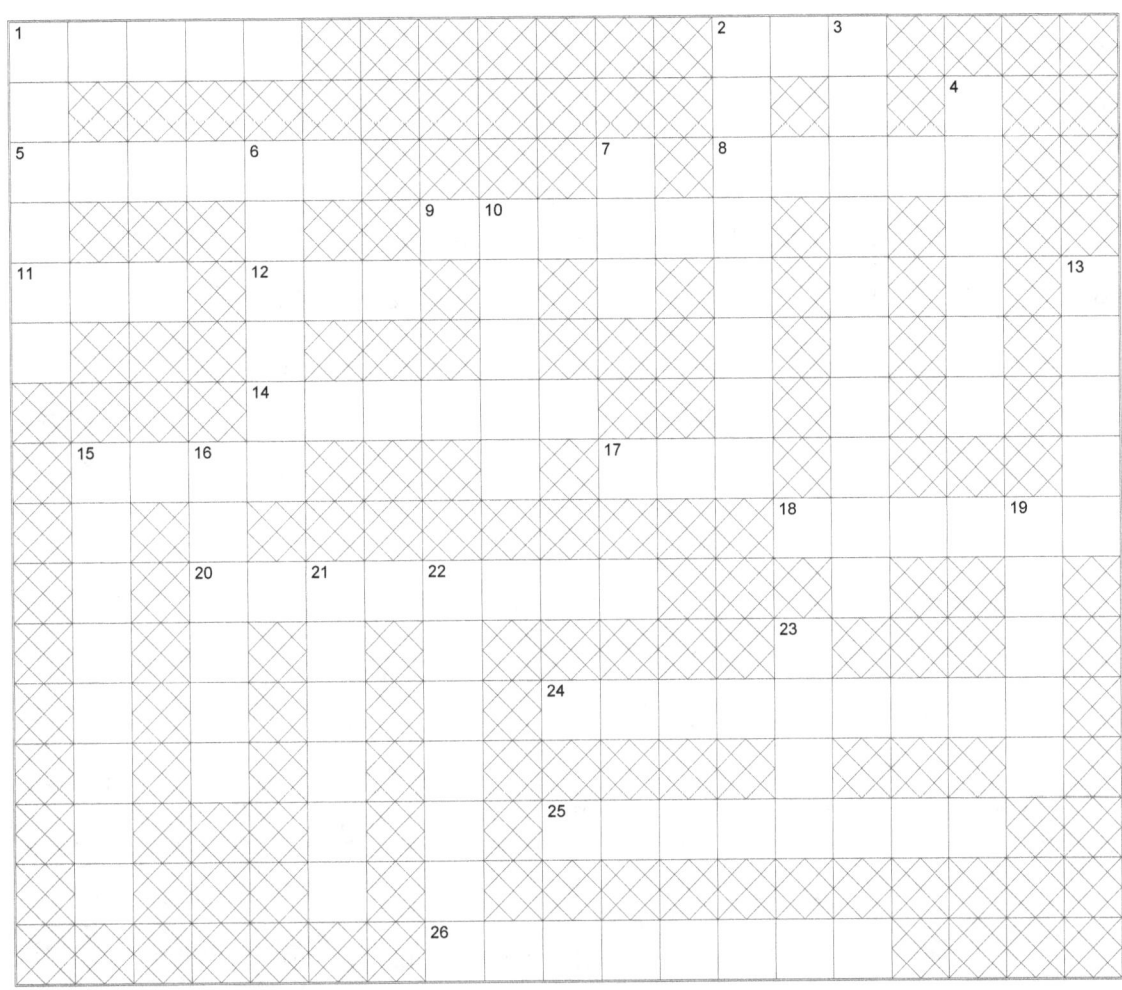

Across
1. Nonnie's new hair coloring job
2. W.E.'s favorite word
5. ____ of Glory; imaginary horse Gilly writes about to W.E.
8. Age when Gilly had seen her mother
9. ____ Street; W.E.'s favorite TV program
11. ___ to one; odds in playground fight
12. Virus all except Gilly caught around Thanksgiving
14. Courtney's mother
15. ____Book; The Holy Bible
17. Number of dollars that fall out from behind encyclopedia
18. Agnes ____ lives with her grandmother
20. National____; test Gilly scored highest on
24. Meanest flower that blows
25. ____ Park; location of foster home in Maryland
26. Mr. ____ eats meals at Maime Trotter's

Down
1. Gilly takes basketball away here
2. Author
3. Poet who wrote about the 'trailing clouds of glory'
4. Gilly's most recent foster parents
6. W.E. learns to do this from Gilly
7. Gilly bought a One-____ticket
10. Miss____; caseworker for Gilly
13. Hundreds of them fill Mr. Randolph's house
15. ____Gilly; nickname main character gives herself
16. Reading group W.E. got promoted to
19. Mr. ____ insists on no fighting at school
21. Amount of money W.E. found for Gilly: ____-four
22. Maime____; hippopotamus of a woman
23. What everyone was offering Gilly

Great Gilly Hopkins Crossword 3 Answer Key

	1 R	I	N	S	E						2 P	O	3 W		
	E										A		O		4 N
	5 C	L	O	6 U	D	S		7 W		8 T	H	R	E	E
	E			E			9 S	E	10 S	A	M	E		D		V
	11 S	I	X		12 F	L	U		L		Y		R		S	I	13 B
	S				E				L				S		W	N	O
				14 N	O	N	N	I	E				O		O	S	O
		15 G	16 O	O	D				17 S		T	E	N		R		K
		R		R										18 S	T	O	19 K	E	S
		U			20 A	21 P	T	22 I	T	U	D	E		H			V
		E			N			H		R				23 H			A
		S			G			I		O		24 D	A	N	D	E	L	I	O	N
		O			E			R		T				L			S
		M						T		T		25 T	H	O	M	P	S	O	N
		E						Y		E							
										26 R	A	N	D	O	L	P	H

Across
1. Nonnie's new hair coloring job
2. W.E.'s favorite word
5. ____ of Glory; imaginary horse Gilly writes about to W.E.
8. Age when Gilly had seen her mother
9. ____ Street; W.E.'s favorite TV program
11. ___ to one; odds in playground fight
12. Virus all except Gilly caught around Thanksgiving
14. Courtney's mother
15. ____Book; The Holy Bible
17. Number of dollars that fall out from behind encyclopedia
18. Agnes ____ lives with her grandmother
20. National____; test Gilly scored highest on
24. Meanest flower that blows
25. ____ Park; location of foster home in Maryland
26. Mr. ____ eats meals at Maime Trotter's

Down
1. Gilly takes basketball away here
2. Author
3. Poet who wrote about the 'trailing clouds of glory'
4. Gilly's most recent foster parents
6. W.E. learns to do this from Gilly
7. Gilly bought a One-____ticket
10. Miss____; caseworker for Gilly
13. Hundreds of them fill Mr. Randolph's house
15. ____Gilly; nickname main character gives herself
16. Reading group W.E. got promoted to
19. Mr. ____ insists on no fighting at school
21. Amount of money W.E. found for Gilly: ___-four
22. Maime____; hippopotamus of a woman
23. What everyone was offering Gilly

Great Gilly Hopkins Crossword 4

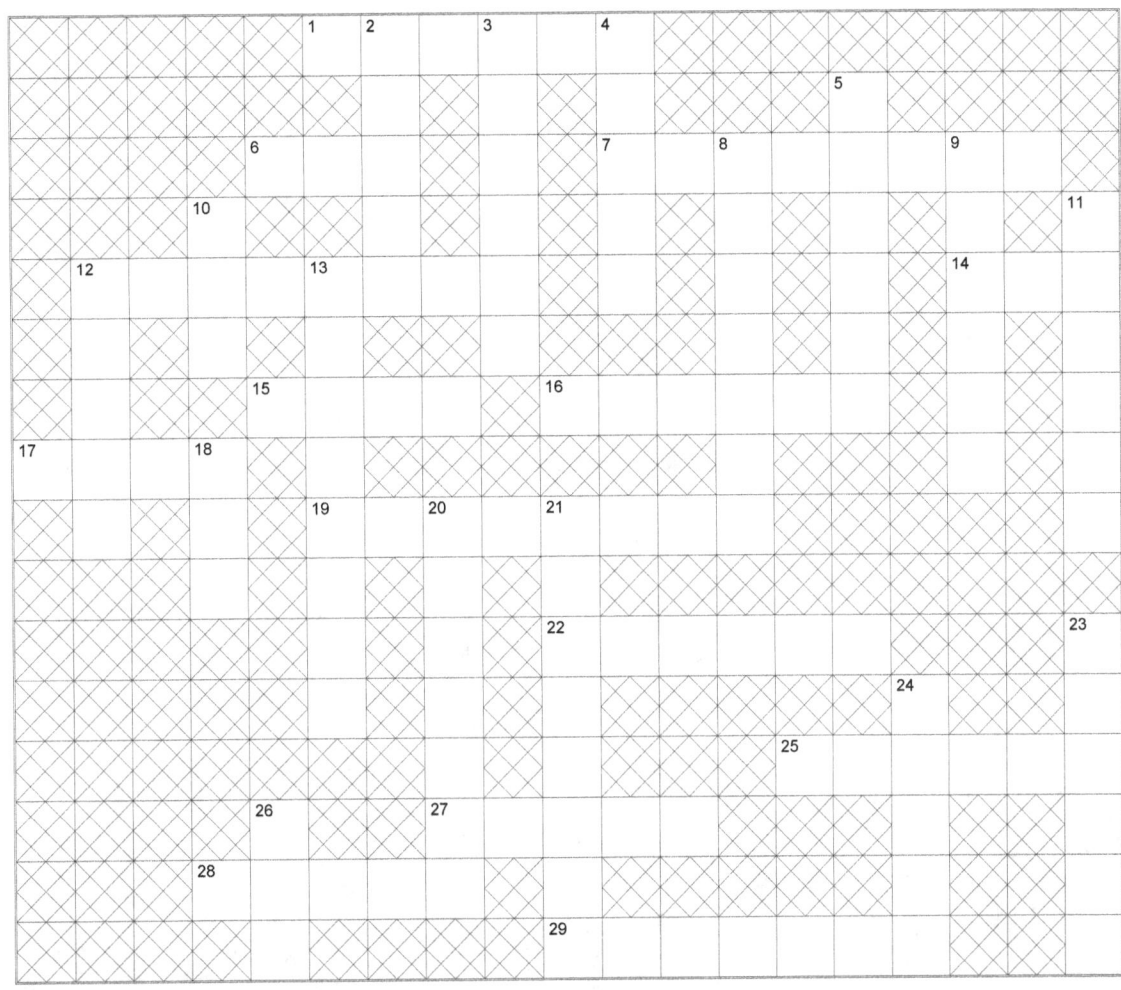

Across
1. Reading group W.E. got promoted to
6. Number of dollars that fall out from behind encyclopedia
7. National____; test Gilly scored highest on
12. Number of years since Nonnie had heard from Courtney
14. Virus all except Gilly caught around Thanksgiving
15. ____Book; The Holy Bible
16. Gilly takes basketball away here
17. What everyone was offering Gilly
19. Author
22. Courtney's mother
25. ____ of Glory; imaginary horse Gilly writes about to W.E.
27. Miss____; caseworker for Gilly
28. ____airplane; 'It sure fly good.'
29. Galadriel____; eleven year-old foster girl

Down
2. Nonnie's new hair coloring job
3. Gilly's most recent foster parents
4. Mr. ____ insists on no fighting at school
5. Agnes ____ lives with her grandmother
8. Author of books Miss Harris sends Gilly
9. W.E. learns to do this from Gilly
10. ___ to one; odds in playground fight
11. ____ gum; Gilly stuck it under left-hand car door handle
12. Age when Gilly had seen her mother
13. ____ Park; location of foster home in Maryland
18. W.E.'s favorite word
20. Maime____; hippopotamus of a woman
21. Mr. ____ eats meals at Maime Trotter's
23. ____ Street; W.E.'s favorite TV program
24. Hundreds of them fill Mr. Randolph's house
26. Gilly bought a One-____ticket

Great Gilly Hopkins Crossword 4 Answer Key

			1 O	2 R	3 A	N	4 G	E					
				I		E		V				5 S	
			6 T	E	N		7 A	P	8 T	I	T	U	D	E
		10 S			S		I		N		O		O		E		11 B
	12 T	H	I	R	13 T	E	E	N		S		L		K		14 F	L	U
		H		X		H		S				K		E		E		B
		R			15 G	O	O	D		16 R	E	C	E	S	S		N		B
17 H	E	L	18 P		M							I				D		L
		E		O			19 P	20 A	T	21 E	R	S	O	N				E
				W			S		R		A							
				O			O		22 N	O	N	N	I	E				23 S
				N			T		D					24 B				E
							T		O				25 C	L	O	U	D	S
				26 W		27 E	L	L	I	S				O				A
			28 P	A	P	E	R			P				K				M
				Y					29 H	O	P	K	I	N	S			E

Across
1. Reading group W.E. got promoted to
6. Number of dollars that fall out from behind encyclopedia
7. National____; test Gilly scored highest on
12. Number of years since Nonnie had heard from Courtney
14. Virus all except Gilly caught around Thanksgiving
15. ____Book; The Holy Bible
16. Gilly takes basketball away here
17. What everyone was offering Gilly
19. Author
22. Courtney's mother
25. ____ of Glory; imaginary horse Gilly writes about to W.E.
27. Miss____; caseworker for Gilly
28. ____airplane; 'It sure fly good.'
29. Galadriel____; eleven year-old foster girl

Down
2. Nonnie's new hair coloring job
3. Gilly's most recent foster parents
4. Mr. ____ insists on no fighting at school
5. Agnes ____ lives with her grandmother
8. Author of books Miss Harris sends Gilly
9. W.E. learns to do this from Gilly
10. ___ to one; odds in playground fight
11. ____ gum; Gilly stuck it under left-hand car door handle
12. Age when Gilly had seen her mother
13. ____ Park; location of foster home in Maryland
18. W.E.'s favorite word
20. Maime____; hippopotamus of a woman
21. Mr. ____ eats meals at Maime Trotter's
23. ____ Street; W.E.'s favorite TV program
24. Hundreds of them fill Mr. Randolph's house
26. Gilly bought a One-____ticket

Great Gilly Hopkins

DANDELION	RANDOLPH	CALIFORNIA	DEFEND	TEN
EVANS	GRUESOME	CLOUDS	RELIGIOUS	BOOKS
FRANCISCO	THOMPSON	FREE SPACE	CLASSROOM	STOKES
RECESS	WORDSWORTH	HARRIS	HOLLYWOOD	SESAME
HOPKINS	SIX	TROTTER	EARNEST	APTITUDE

Great Gilly Hopkins

THIRTY	NONNIE	PAPER	FLU	RINSE
ORANGE	CHADWELL	NEVINS	THREE	ELLIS
BUBBLE	JACKSON	FREE SPACE	INSCRIPTION	TOLKEIN
THIRTEEN	PATERSON	DULLES	GOOD	HELP
POW	BLACK	APTITUDE	EARNEST	TROTTER

Great Gilly Hopkins

FRANCISCO	THIRTY	FLU	DEFEND	TROTTER
SIX	DANDELION	RUTHERFORD	RINSE	GRUESOME
PATERSON	RELIGIOUS	FREE SPACE	THREE	HOPKINS
THOMPSON	DULLES	NEVINS	STOKES	GOOD
TEN	APTITUDE	POW	WORDSWORTH	ELLIS

Great Gilly Hopkins

THIRTEEN	BLACK	PAPER	NONNIE	EARNEST
EVANS	WAY	BOOKS	CHADWELL	JACKSON
HOLLYWOOD	TOLKEIN	FREE SPACE	ORANGE	BUBBLE
CLASSROOM	CALIFORNIA	CLOUDS	INSCRIPTION	SESAME
RANDOLPH	HELP	ELLIS	WORDSWORTH	POW

Great Gilly Hopkins

BOOKS	THIRTEEN	HARRIS	INSCRIPTION	DEFEND
TEN	EARNEST	GOOD	TOLKEIN	STOKES
WAY	EVANS	FREE SPACE	PATERSON	CLASSROOM
DULLES	NONNIE	CHADWELL	FRANCISCO	HOPKINS
APTITUDE	HOLLYWOOD	GRUESOME	RECESS	WORDSWORTH

Great Gilly Hopkins

RINSE	DANDELION	RUTHERFORD	CALIFORNIA	CLOUDS
TROTTER	ELLIS	THIRTY	PAPER	BLACK
NEVINS	SESAME	FREE SPACE	SIX	BUBBLE
THOMPSON	FLU	RANDOLPH	THREE	HELP
POW	ORANGE	WORDSWORTH	RECESS	GRUESOME

Great Gilly Hopkins

HARRIS	GOOD	BOOKS	TOLKEIN	EARNEST
DULLES	THOMPSON	HELP	TEN	SIX
ELLIS	EVANS	FREE SPACE	PATERSON	RELIGIOUS
THIRTEEN	CHADWELL	NEVINS	STOKES	RUTHERFORD
INSCRIPTION	HOLLYWOOD	PAPER	TROTTER	DANDELION

Great Gilly Hopkins

WAY	CALIFORNIA	RECESS	POW	SESAME
CLOUDS	CLASSROOM	JACKSON	RINSE	NONNIE
BLACK	GRUESOME	FREE SPACE	THIRTY	HOPKINS
THREE	APTITUDE	BUBBLE	RANDOLPH	ORANGE
WORDSWORTH	DEFEND	DANDELION	TROTTER	PAPER

Great Gilly Hopkins

THREE	THIRTEEN	RINSE	RELIGIOUS	CHADWELL
CLASSROOM	CLOUDS	BUBBLE	NONNIE	FLU
SESAME	JACKSON	FREE SPACE	WORDSWORTH	THIRTY
RUTHERFORD	HOLLYWOOD	NEVINS	WAY	APTITUDE
TROTTER	DULLES	ELLIS	TEN	STOKES

Great Gilly Hopkins

POW	THOMPSON	HOPKINS	GRUESOME	DANDELION
FRANCISCO	DEFEND	HELP	BOOKS	ORANGE
PAPER	RECESS	FREE SPACE	BLACK	EVANS
GOOD	CALIFORNIA	TOLKEIN	EARNEST	SIX
RANDOLPH	HARRIS	STOKES	TEN	ELLIS

Great Gilly Hopkins

RUTHERFORD	TROTTER	THOMPSON	JACKSON	SESAME
INSCRIPTION	ORANGE	CALIFORNIA	HARRIS	GRUESOME
CHADWELL	NEVINS	FREE SPACE	POW	WAY
RINSE	FRANCISCO	APTITUDE	THIRTY	DANDELION
FLU	BLACK	HOLLYWOOD	WORDSWORTH	HELP

Great Gilly Hopkins

BOOKS	TEN	DULLES	THIRTEEN	EVANS
GOOD	HOPKINS	PATERSON	SIX	CLASSROOM
RELIGIOUS	CLOUDS	FREE SPACE	STOKES	ELLIS
EARNEST	NONNIE	RANDOLPH	DEFEND	RECESS
TOLKEIN	BUBBLE	HELP	WORDSWORTH	HOLLYWOOD

Great Gilly Hopkins

RUTHERFORD	PATERSON	POW	THOMPSON	PAPER
TEN	EVANS	BLACK	RINSE	BOOKS
JACKSON	ELLIS	FREE SPACE	APTITUDE	GOOD
DANDELION	SESAME	DULLES	FRANCISCO	TROTTER
CALIFORNIA	DEFEND	FLU	HELP	INSCRIPTION

Great Gilly Hopkins

SIX	THIRTEEN	WORDSWORTH	ORANGE	GRUESOME
HOPKINS	RELIGIOUS	THIRTY	TOLKEIN	BUBBLE
HARRIS	CHADWELL	FREE SPACE	NEVINS	CLOUDS
HOLLYWOOD	RANDOLPH	NONNIE	WAY	RECESS
THREE	STOKES	INSCRIPTION	HELP	FLU

Great Gilly Hopkins

NONNIE	EVANS	APTITUDE	TOLKEIN	THIRTEEN
PATERSON	THOMPSON	RINSE	HARRIS	ORANGE
RELIGIOUS	WAY	FREE SPACE	FLU	BOOKS
NEVINS	POW	STOKES	HELP	BLACK
HOPKINS	SESAME	ELLIS	GOOD	CLOUDS

Great Gilly Hopkins

THREE	HOLLYWOOD	FRANCISCO	INSCRIPTION	RECESS
RUTHERFORD	GRUESOME	RANDOLPH	WORDSWORTH	BUBBLE
CALIFORNIA	SIX	FREE SPACE	CHADWELL	DEFEND
PAPER	TROTTER	DULLES	DANDELION	EARNEST
CLASSROOM	JACKSON	CLOUDS	GOOD	ELLIS

Great Gilly Hopkins

CHADWELL	TEN	CLASSROOM	BUBBLE	JACKSON
RUTHERFORD	STOKES	RELIGIOUS	PAPER	WAY
RANDOLPH	CALIFORNIA	FREE SPACE	FLU	HELP
INSCRIPTION	ELLIS	BOOKS	GOOD	POW
THIRTEEN	HOPKINS	CLOUDS	DULLES	WORDSWORTH

Great Gilly Hopkins

SIX	TROTTER	RINSE	APTITUDE	THIRTY
SESAME	RECESS	NONNIE	NEVINS	GRUESOME
HOLLYWOOD	DANDELION	FREE SPACE	THREE	DEFEND
HARRIS	TOLKEIN	EARNEST	EVANS	BLACK
ORANGE	THOMPSON	WORDSWORTH	DULLES	CLOUDS

Great Gilly Hopkins

HOPKINS	TROTTER	TOLKEIN	TEN	RECESS
RANDOLPH	APTITUDE	WAY	BOOKS	FRANCISCO
PAPER	HELP	FREE SPACE	JACKSON	GRUESOME
RELIGIOUS	FLU	ORANGE	CALIFORNIA	EARNEST
POW	THIRTY	CHADWELL	RUTHERFORD	SESAME

Great Gilly Hopkins

BLACK	INSCRIPTION	STOKES	NEVINS	HARRIS
DULLES	CLASSROOM	EVANS	HOLLYWOOD	THOMPSON
WORDSWORTH	GOOD	FREE SPACE	CLOUDS	DANDELION
DEFEND	RINSE	SIX	ELLIS	PATERSON
NONNIE	BUBBLE	SESAME	RUTHERFORD	CHADWELL

Great Gilly Hopkins

HELP	RELIGIOUS	DANDELION	CLOUDS	JACKSON
NONNIE	NEVINS	THREE	THIRTEEN	HOLLYWOOD
BUBBLE	THIRTY	FREE SPACE	RUTHERFORD	ELLIS
EARNEST	BOOKS	TROTTER	FLU	DEFEND
RANDOLPH	PATERSON	FRANCISCO	PAPER	CLASSROOM

Great Gilly Hopkins

INSCRIPTION	EVANS	HOPKINS	ORANGE	HARRIS
WAY	GRUESOME	CALIFORNIA	POW	RINSE
SESAME	TOLKEIN	FREE SPACE	STOKES	THOMPSON
GOOD	CHADWELL	APTITUDE	SIX	BLACK
DULLES	TEN	CLASSROOM	PAPER	FRANCISCO

Great Gilly Hopkins

GRUESOME	APTITUDE	PATERSON	STOKES	NEVINS
THIRTY	ORANGE	POW	ELLIS	INSCRIPTION
HELP	FRANCISCO	FREE SPACE	BOOKS	RANDOLPH
BLACK	BUBBLE	TOLKEIN	THREE	RECESS
DEFEND	PAPER	THIRTEEN	HOLLYWOOD	RINSE

Great Gilly Hopkins

SESAME	FLU	NONNIE	DANDELION	THOMPSON
RUTHERFORD	CHADWELL	CALIFORNIA	EARNEST	JACKSON
WAY	WORDSWORTH	FREE SPACE	TROTTER	CLOUDS
GOOD	DULLES	HOPKINS	RELIGIOUS	HARRIS
SIX	CLASSROOM	RINSE	HOLLYWOOD	THIRTEEN

Great Gilly Hopkins

THOMPSON	SIX	HOLLYWOOD	RUTHERFORD	TEN
STOKES	THIRTY	DEFEND	WORDSWORTH	ELLIS
SESAME	EVANS	FREE SPACE	POW	NEVINS
HOPKINS	APTITUDE	PATERSON	TROTTER	WAY
RINSE	FRANCISCO	HARRIS	ORANGE	INSCRIPTION

Great Gilly Hopkins

CALIFORNIA	NONNIE	TOLKEIN	CLASSROOM	RECESS
BLACK	GOOD	DULLES	GRUESOME	CLOUDS
RANDOLPH	THIRTEEN	FREE SPACE	EARNEST	DANDELION
PAPER	HELP	BOOKS	JACKSON	FLU
BUBBLE	RELIGIOUS	INSCRIPTION	ORANGE	HARRIS

Great Gilly Hopkins

CALIFORNIA	THOMPSON	GRUESOME	TEN	RINSE
PAPER	TROTTER	PATERSON	BUBBLE	APTITUDE
BLACK	RECESS	FREE SPACE	WAY	NEVINS
CLASSROOM	CLOUDS	EARNEST	RELIGIOUS	FLU
CHADWELL	HOLLYWOOD	TOLKEIN	POW	RANDOLPH

Great Gilly Hopkins

INSCRIPTION	JACKSON	GOOD	HARRIS	SESAME
RUTHERFORD	BOOKS	THREE	EVANS	NONNIE
THIRTY	SIX	FREE SPACE	HOPKINS	HELP
STOKES	THIRTEEN	ORANGE	FRANCISCO	DANDELION
WORDSWORTH	ELLIS	RANDOLPH	POW	TOLKEIN

Great Gilly Hopkins

WORDSWORTH	HELP	HARRIS	BUBBLE	RUTHERFORD
PAPER	RELIGIOUS	TOLKEIN	WAY	NONNIE
CHADWELL	RINSE	FREE SPACE	TROTTER	CLOUDS
THIRTY	DANDELION	GOOD	APTITUDE	FRANCISCO
ORANGE	CLASSROOM	JACKSON	SESAME	EARNEST

Great Gilly Hopkins

THOMPSON	STOKES	BLACK	GRUESOME	CALIFORNIA
DEFEND	RANDOLPH	PATERSON	FLU	POW
NEVINS	THIRTEEN	FREE SPACE	ELLIS	THREE
INSCRIPTION	TEN	RECESS	BOOKS	HOLLYWOOD
EVANS	DULLES	EARNEST	SESAME	JACKSON

Great Gilly Hopkins

HARRIS	SIX	EVANS	BLACK	RINSE
RELIGIOUS	THOMPSON	TROTTER	THIRTEEN	RECESS
GOOD	THIRTY	FREE SPACE	HOLLYWOOD	NONNIE
THREE	GRUESOME	EARNEST	WORDSWORTH	TOLKEIN
HOPKINS	NEVINS	APTITUDE	STOKES	BOOKS

Great Gilly Hopkins

FRANCISCO	FLU	CLOUDS	CALIFORNIA	INSCRIPTION
PATERSON	ELLIS	TEN	WAY	POW
DULLES	CLASSROOM	FREE SPACE	DANDELION	CHADWELL
BUBBLE	ORANGE	HELP	DEFEND	JACKSON
SESAME	PAPER	BOOKS	STOKES	APTITUDE

Great Gilly Hopkins Vocabulary Word List

No.	Word	Clue/Definition
1.	AGONY	Misery
2.	ANOINTED	Dedicated
3.	ANONYMOUS	Unsigned
4.	APPALLING	Shocking
5.	APPARITION	Ghost
6.	AUDIBLE	Hearable
7.	BARRACUDA	Predatory fish
8.	BELLIGERENTLY	With hostility
9.	BENIGNLY	Favorably
10.	CANOPIED	Decoratively covered between bedposts
11.	CHANDELIER	Glass light hanging from ceiling
12.	CONFIRMED	Proved
13.	CULINARY	Cooking
14.	DELECTABLE	Delicious
15.	DELINQUENCY	Neglect; wrong doing
16.	DIVERTED	Changed; distracted
17.	ELABORATELY	With great detail
18.	EMBRACE	Hug
19.	EMBROIDERED	Having needlework
20.	EMPHATICALLY	Intensely
21.	ENGRAVED	Impressed deeply
22.	ENGULFED	Flooded
23.	ENTHRALLED	Fascinated
24.	EXPANSE	Stretch
25.	FANATIC	Maniac
26.	FEEBLE	Weak
27.	FLIRTATION	Easing
28.	FLUTED	Having grooves
29.	FRACAS	Uproar
30.	FUTILE	Useless
31.	GAUDIEST	Flashiest
32.	HEFTING	Lifting
33.	IMBECILE	Dimwit; moron
34.	INCOMPETENCE	Inability; failing
35.	INEXORABLY	Unable to be stopped
36.	IRRITABILITY	Testiness
37.	KALEIDOSCOPIC	Brilliant
38.	LABORIOUSLY	With great difficulty
39.	LADEN	Loaded down
40.	LEERING	Glaring
41.	MONOGRAMMED	Designed with letters
42.	OBLIGINGLY	In an obeying manner
43.	OBSCENITY	Swearing
44.	PERPETUAL	Endless
45.	PIOUSLY	In a holy manner
46.	PSYCHOLOGISTS	Therapists
47.	QUAVERING	Trembling
48.	RELENTLESSLY	Steadily
49.	REPERTORY	Collection
50.	RIFFLED	Searched
51.	SALVAGE	Rescue; save

Great Gilly Hopkins Vocabulary Word List Continued

No.	Word	Clue/Definition
52.	SEETHED	Raged; fumed
53.	SELF-RIGHTEOUS	Pure
54.	STRICKEN	Troubled
55.	SUBMISSION	Meekness; surrender
56.	TENTATIVELY	Uncertainly
57.	TRIFLED	Toyed or played with
58.	VARIATIONS	Varieties
59.	VENGEANCE	Revenge
60.	WOEFULLY	Sadly

Great Gilly Hopkins Vocabulary Fill In The Blank 1

_____ 1. with great difficulty

_____ 2. decoratively covered between the tops of bedposts

_____ 3. shocking

_____ 4. dedicated

_____ 5. collection

_____ 6. endless

_____ 7. uproar

_____ 8. teasing

_____ 9. meekness; surrender

_____ 10. stretch

_____ 11. impressed deeply

_____ 12. having needlework

_____ 13. moron; dimwit

_____ 14. unable to stop

_____ 15. predatory fish

_____ 16. proved

_____ 17. rescue; save

_____ 18. glass light hanging from the ceiling

_____ 19. glaring

_____ 20. in an obeying manner

Great Gilly Hopkins Vocabulary Fill In The Blank 1 Answer Key

LABORIOUSLY	1. with great difficulty
CANOPIED	2. decoratively covered between the tops of bedposts
APPALLING	3. shocking
ANOINTED	4. dedicated
REPERTORY	5. collection
PERPETUAL	6. endless
FRACAS	7. uproar
FLIRTATION	8. teasing
SUBMISSION	9. meekness; surrender
EXPANSE	10. stretch
ENGRAVED	11. impressed deeply
EMBROIDERED	12. having needlework
IMBECILE	13. moron; dimwit
INEXORABLY	14. unable to stop
BARRACUDA	15. predatory fish
CONFIRMED	16. proved
SALVAGE	17. rescue; save
CHANDELIER	18. glass light hanging from the ceiling
LEERING	19. glaring
OBLIGINGLY	20. in an obeying manner

Great Gilly Hopkins Vocabulary Fill In The Blank 2

_____ 1. unsigned

_____ 2. glaring

_____ 3. variety

_____ 4. searched

_____ 5. teasing

_____ 6. useless

_____ 7. brilliant

_____ 8. with great difficulty

_____ 9. shocking

_____ 10. changed; distracted

_____ 11. delicious

_____ 12. impressed deeply

_____ 13. dedicated

_____ 14. meekness; surrender

_____ 15. toyed or played with

_____ 16. therapists

_____ 17. revenge

_____ 18. with hosility

_____ 19. raged; fumed

_____ 20. with great detail

Great Gilly Hopkins Vocabulary Fill In The Blank 2 Answer Key

ANONYMOUS	1. unsigned
LEERING	2. glaring
VARIATIONS	3. variety
RIFFLED	4. searched
FLIRTATION	5. teasing
FUTILE	6. useless
KALEIDOSCOPIC	7. brilliant
LABORIOUSLY	8. with great difficulty
APPALLING	9. shocking
DIVERTED	10. changed; distracted
DELECTABLE	11. delicious
ENGRAVED	12. impressed deeply
ANOINTED	13. dedicated
SUBMISSION	14. meekness; surrender
TRIFLED	15. toyed or played with
PSYCHOLOGISTS	16. therapists
VENGEANCE	17. revenge
BELLIGERENTLY	18. with hosility
SEETHED	19. raged; fumed
ELABORATELY	20. with great detail

Great Gilly Hopkins Vocabulary Fill In The Blank 3

_____ 1. steadily

_____ 2. pure

_____ 3. concerning cooking

_____ 4. shocking

_____ 5. lifting

_____ 6. glaring

_____ 7. rescue; save

_____ 8. therapists

_____ 9. raged; fumed

_____ 10. delicious

_____ 11. proved

_____ 12. in a holy manner

_____ 13. loaded down

_____ 14. maniac

_____ 15. revenge

_____ 16. favorably

_____ 17. with great difficulty

_____ 18. weak

_____ 19. hearable

_____ 20. unable to stop

Great Gilly Hopkins Vocabulary Fill In The Blank 3 Answer Key

RELENTLESSLY	1. steadily
SELF-RIGHTEOUS	2. pure
CULINARY	3. concerning cooking
APPALLING	4. shocking
HEFTING	5. lifting
LEERING	6. glaring
SALVAGE	7. rescue; save
PSYCHOLOGISTS	8. therapists
SEETHED	9. raged; fumed
DELECTABLE	10. delicious
CONFIRMED	11. proved
PIOUSLY	12. in a holy manner
LADEN	13. loaded down
FANATIC	14. maniac
VENGEANCE	15. revenge
BENIGNLY	16. favorably
LABORIOUSLY	17. with great difficulty
FEEBLE	18. weak
AUDIBLE	19. hearable
INEXORABLY	20. unable to stop

Great Gilly Hopkins Vocabulary Fill In The Blank 4

_____ 1. lifting

_____ 2. favorably

_____ 3. hearable

_____ 4. toyed or played with

_____ 5. glass light hanging from the ceiling

_____ 6. trembling

_____ 7. with great difficulty

_____ 8. testiness

_____ 9. with uncertainty

_____ 10. ghost

_____ 11. uproar

_____ 12. unable to stop

_____ 13. useless

_____ 14. therapists

_____ 15. collection

_____ 16. revenge

_____ 17. searched

_____ 18. designed with letters

_____ 19. meekness; surrender

_____ 20. proved

Great Gilly Hopkins Vocabulary Fill In The Blank 4 Answer Key

HEFTING	1. lifting
BENIGNLY	2. favorably
AUDIBLE	3. hearable
TRIFLED	4. toyed or played with
CHANDELIER	5. glass light hanging from the ceiling
QUAVERING	6. trembling
LABORIOUSLY	7. with great difficulty
IRRITABILITY	8. testiness
TENTATIVELY	9. with uncertainty
APPARITION	10. ghost
FRACAS	11. uproar
INEXORABLY	12. unable to stop
FUTILE	13. useless
PSYCHOLOGISTS	14. therapists
REPERTORY	15. collection
VENGEANCE	16. revenge
RIFFLED	17. searched
MONOGRAMMED	18. designed with letters
SUBMISSION	19. meekness; surrender
CONFIRMED	20. proved

Great Gilly Hopkins Vocabulary Matching 1

___ 1. LEERING   A. ghost
___ 2. SALVAGE   B. pure
___ 3. FRACAS   C. weak
___ 4. DELECTABLE   D. inability; failing
___ 5. PSYCHOLOGISTS   E. designed with letters
___ 6. INCOMPETENCE   F. steadily
___ 7. MONOGRAMMED   G. maniac
___ 8. SUBMISSION   H. with uncertainty
___ 9. BARRACUDA   I. unable to stop
___ 10. SELF-RIGHTEOUS   J. predatory fish
___ 11. FEEBLE   K. shocking
___ 12. APPARITION   L. testiness
___ 13. ELABORATELY   M. trembling
___ 14. QUAVERING   N. delicious
___ 15. REPERTORY   O. rescue; save
___ 16. RELENTLESSLY   P. glaring
___ 17. APPALLING   Q. hug
___ 18. INEXORABLY   R. collection
___ 19. FLIRTATION   S. with great detail
___ 20. FANATIC   T. meekness; surrender
___ 21. IRRITABILITY   U. loaded down
___ 22. TENTATIVELY   V. therapists
___ 23. LADEN   W. uproar
___ 24. VARIATIONS   X. teasing
___ 25. EMBRACE   Y. variety

Great Gilly Hopkins Vocabulary Matching 1 Answer Key

P - 1. LEERING   A. ghost
O - 2. SALVAGE   B. pure
W - 3. FRACAS   C. weak
N - 4. DELECTABLE   D. inability; failing
V - 5. PSYCHOLOGISTS   E. designed with letters
D - 6. INCOMPETENCE   F. steadily
E - 7. MONOGRAMMED   G. maniac
T - 8. SUBMISSION   H. with uncertainty
J - 9. BARRACUDA   I. unable to stop
B - 10. SELF-RIGHTEOUS J. predatory fish
C - 11. FEEBLE   K. shocking
A - 12. APPARITION   L. testiness
S - 13. ELABORATELY   M. trembling
M - 14. QUAVERING   N. delicious
R - 15. REPERTORY   O. rescue; save
F - 16. RELENTLESSLY   P. glaring
K - 17. APPALLING   Q. hug
I - 18. INEXORABLY   R. collection
X - 19. FLIRTATION   S. with great detail
G - 20. FANATIC   T. meekness; surrender
L - 21. IRRITABILITY   U. loaded down
H - 22. TENTATIVELY   V. therapists
U - 23. LADEN   W. uproar
Y - 24. VARIATIONS   X. teasing
Q - 25. EMBRACE   Y. variety

Great Gilly Hopkins Vocabulary Matching 2

___ 1. ENGRAVED   A. hearable
___ 2. WOEFULLY   B. impressed deeply
___ 3. SELF-RIGHTEOUS   C. flashiest
___ 4. ENTHRALLED   D. brilliant
___ 5. FEEBLE   E. troubled
___ 6. EMPHATICALLY   F. delicious
___ 7. AUDIBLE   G. intensely
___ 8. STRICKEN   H. steadily
___ 9. SUBMISSION   I. in an obeying manner
___10. RELENTLESSLY   J. with uncertainty
___11. KALEIDOSCOPIC   K. glass light hanging from the ceiling
___12. TRIFLED   L. inability; failing
___13. CONFIRMED   M. ghost
___14. DELECTABLE   N. misery
___15. APPARITION   O. weak
___16. AGONY   P. shocking
___17. VARIATIONS   Q. loaded down
___18. TENTATIVELY   R. proved
___19. ENGULFED   S. flooded
___20. LADEN   T. toyed or played with
___21. INCOMPETENCE   U. sadly
___22. CHANDELIER   V. pure
___23. GAUDIEST   W. variety
___24. OBLIGINGLY   X. meekness; surrender
___25. APPALLING   Y. fascinated

Great Gilly Hopkins Vocabulary Matching 2 Answer Key

B - 1. ENGRAVED   A. hearable
U - 2. WOEFULLY   B. impressed deeply
V - 3. SELF-RIGHTEOUS   C. flashiest
Y - 4. ENTHRALLED   D. brilliant
O - 5. FEEBLE   E. troubled
G - 6. EMPHATICALLY   F. delicious
A - 7. AUDIBLE   G. intensely
E - 8. STRICKEN   H. steadily
X - 9. SUBMISSION   I. in an obeying manner
H -10. RELENTLESSLY   J. with uncertainty
D -11. KALEIDOSCOPIC   K. glass light hanging from the ceiling
T -12. TRIFLED   L. inability; failing
R -13. CONFIRMED   M. ghost
F -14. DELECTABLE   N. misery
M -15. APPARITION   O. weak
N -16. AGONY   P. shocking
W -17. VARIATIONS   Q. loaded down
J -18. TENTATIVELY   R. proved
S -19. ENGULFED   S. flooded
Q -20. LADEN   T. toyed or played with
L -21. INCOMPETENCE   U. sadly
K -22. CHANDELIER   V. pure
C -23. GAUDIEST   W. variety
I -24. OBLIGINGLY   X. meekness; surrender
P -25. APPALLING   Y. fascinated

Great Gilly Hopkins Vocabulary Matching 3

___ 1. LABORIOUSLY   A. flooded
___ 2. RIFFLED   B. hearable
___ 3. OBLIGINGLY   C. with great detail
___ 4. ENGULFED   D. sadly
___ 5. SALVAGE   E. in a holy manner
___ 6. REPERTORY   F. flashiest
___ 7. ENTHRALLED   G. weak
___ 8. FLIRTATION   H. testiness
___ 9. DIVERTED   I. therapists
___10. OBSCENITY   J. proved
___11. INCOMPETENCE   K. rescue; save
___12. HEFTING   L. in an obeying manner
___13. PIOUSLY   M. uproar
___14. WOEFULLY   N. dedicated
___15. CULINARY   O. lifting
___16. ANOINTED   P. inability; failing
___17. PSYCHOLOGISTS   Q. teasing
___18. CONFIRMED   R. searched
___19. IMBECILE   S. with great difficulty
___20. ELABORATELY   T. changed; distracted
___21. FRACAS   U. swearing
___22. FEEBLE   V. moron; dimwit
___23. GAUDIEST   W. fascinated
___24. IRRITABILITY   X. collection
___25. AUDIBLE   Y. concerning cooking

Great Gilly Hopkins Vocabulary Matching 3 Answer Key

S - 1.	LABORIOUSLY	A.	flooded
R - 2.	RIFFLED	B.	hearable
L - 3.	OBLIGINGLY	C.	with great detail
A - 4.	ENGULFED	D.	sadly
K - 5.	SALVAGE	E.	in a holy manner
X - 6.	REPERTORY	F.	flashiest
W - 7.	ENTHRALLED	G.	weak
Q - 8.	FLIRTATION	H.	testiness
T - 9.	DIVERTED	I.	therapists
U - 10.	OBSCENITY	J.	proved
P - 11.	INCOMPETENCE	K.	rescue; save
O - 12.	HEFTING	L.	in an obeying manner
E - 13.	PIOUSLY	M.	uproar
D - 14.	WOEFULLY	N.	dedicated
Y - 15.	CULINARY	O.	lifting
N - 16.	ANOINTED	P.	inability; failing
I - 17.	PSYCHOLOGISTS	Q.	teasing
J - 18.	CONFIRMED	R.	searched
V - 19.	IMBECILE	S.	with great difficulty
C - 20.	ELABORATELY	T.	changed; distracted
M - 21.	FRACAS	U.	swearing
G - 22.	FEEBLE	V.	moron; dimwit
F - 23.	GAUDIEST	W.	fascinated
H - 24.	IRRITABILITY	X.	collection
B - 25.	AUDIBLE	Y.	concerning cooking

Great Gilly Hopkins Vocabulary Matching 4

___ 1. FRACAS   A. meekness; surrender
___ 2. MONOGRAMMED   B. designed with letters
___ 3. CONFIRMED   C. with great difficulty
___ 4. FUTILE   D. ghost
___ 5. LABORIOUSLY   E. with great detail
___ 6. INEXORABLY   F. predatory fish
___ 7. INCOMPETENCE   G. hug
___ 8. SUBMISSION   H. hearable
___ 9. ENTHRALLED   I. inability; failing
___10. GAUDIEST   J. fascinated
___11. LEERING   K. trembling
___12. EMBRACE   L. revenge
___13. VENGEANCE   M. with hosility
___14. BENIGNLY   N. uproar
___15. AUDIBLE   O. favorably
___16. APPALLING   P. weak
___17. BELLIGERENTLY   Q. proved
___18. EXPANSE   R. changed; distracted
___19. DIVERTED   S. unable to stop
___20. APPARITION   T. flashiest
___21. FEEBLE   U. shocking
___22. BARRACUDA   V. collection
___23. QUAVERING   W. glaring
___24. ELABORATELY   X. stretch
___25. REPERTORY   Y. useless

Great Gilly Hopkins Vocabulary Matching 4 Answer Key

N - 1. FRACAS   A. meekness; surrender
B - 2. MONOGRAMMED   B. designed with letters
Q - 3. CONFIRMED   C. with great difficulty
Y - 4. FUTILE   D. ghost
C - 5. LABORIOUSLY   E. with great detail
S - 6. INEXORABLY   F. predatory fish
I - 7. INCOMPETENCE   G. hug
A - 8. SUBMISSION   H. hearable
J - 9. ENTHRALLED   I. inability; failing
T - 10. GAUDIEST   J. fascinated
W - 11. LEERING   K. trembling
G - 12. EMBRACE   L. revenge
L - 13. VENGEANCE   M. with hosility
O - 14. BENIGNLY   N. uproar
H - 15. AUDIBLE   O. favorably
U - 16. APPALLING   P. weak
M - 17. BELLIGERENTLY   Q. proved
X - 18. EXPANSE   R. changed; distracted
R - 19. DIVERTED   S. unable to stop
D - 20. APPARITION   T. flashiest
P - 21. FEEBLE   U. shocking
F - 22. BARRACUDA   V. collection
K - 23. QUAVERING   W. glaring
E - 24. ELABORATELY   X. stretch
V - 25. REPERTORY   Y. useless

Great Gilly Hopkins Vocabulary Magic Squares 1

Match the definition with the vocabulary word. Put your answers in the magic squares below. When your answers are correct, all columns and rows will add to the same number.

A. ENGULFED
B. INEXORABLY
C. RIFFLED
D. ANONYMOUS
E. CHANDELIER
F. OBLIGINGLY
G. CANOPIED
H. EMBROIDERED
I. FEEBLE
J. FUTILE
K. LADEN
L. IMBECILE
M. ANOINTED
N. SELF-RIGHTEOUS
O. SUBMISSION
P. STRICKEN

1. meekness; surrender
2. unsigned
3. useless
4. glass light hanging from the ceiling
5. weak
6. in an obeying manner
7. troubled
8. searched
9. having needlework
10. loaded down
11. flooded
12. pure
13. unable to stop
14. dedicated
15. decoratively covered between the tops of bedposts
16. moron; dimwit

A=	B=	C=	D=
E=	F=	G=	H=
I=	J=	K=	L=
M=	N=	O=	P=

Copyrighted

Great Gilly Hopkins Vocabulary Magic Squares 1 Answer Key

Match the definition with the vocabulary word. Put your answers in the magic squares below. When your answers are correct, all columns and rows will add to the same number.

A. ENGULFED
B. INEXORABLY
C. RIFFLED
D. ANONYMOUS
E. CHANDELIER
F. OBLIGINGLY
G. CANOPIED
H. EMBROIDERED
I. FEEBLE
J. FUTILE
K. LADEN
L. IMBECILE
M. ANOINTED
N. SELF-RIGHTEOUS
O. SUBMISSION
P. STRICKEN

1. meekness; surrender
2. unsigned
3. useless
4. glass light hanging from the ceiling
5. weak
6. in an obeying manner
7. troubled
8. searched
9. having needlework
10. loaded down
11. flooded
12. pure
13. unable to stop
14. dedicated
15. decoratively covered between the tops of bedposts
16. moron; dimwit

A=11	B=13	C=8	D=2
E=4	F=6	G=15	H=9
I=5	J=3	K=10	L=16
M=14	N=12	O=1	P=7

Great Gilly Hopkins Vocabulary Magic Squares 2

Match the definition with the vocabulary word. Put your answers in the magic squares below. When your answers are correct, all columns and rows will add to the same number.

A. OBLIGINGLY
B. INCOMPETENCE
C. BARRACUDA
D. LEERING
E. OBSCENITY
F. VARIATIONS
G. FUTILE
H. ENTHRALLED
I. TRIFLED
J. REPERTORY
K. CONFIRMED
L. DIVERTED
M. SEETHED
N. RIFFLED
O. ANONYMOUS
P. PIOUSLY

1. raged; fumed
2. variety
3. fascinated
4. unsigned
5. changed; distracted
6. predatory fish
7. in an obeying manner
8. collection
9. proved
10. glaring
11. inability; failing
12. toyed or played with
13. searched
14. swearing
15. useless
16. in a holy manner

A=	B=	C=	D=
E=	F=	G=	H=
I=	J=	K=	L=
M=	N=	O=	P=

81
Copyrighted

Great Gilly Hopkins Vocabulary Magic Squares 2 Answer Key

Match the definition with the vocabulary word. Put your answers in the magic squares below. When your answers are correct, all columns and rows will add to the same number.

A. OBLIGINGLY
B. INCOMPETENCE
C. BARRACUDA
D. LEERING
E. OBSCENITY
F. VARIATIONS
G. FUTILE
H. ENTHRALLED
I. TRIFLED
J. REPERTORY
K. CONFIRMED
L. DIVERTED
M. SEETHED
N. RIFFLED
O. ANONYMOUS
P. PIOUSLY

1. raged; fumed
2. variety
3. fascinated
4. unsigned
5. changed; distracted
6. predatory fish
7. in an obeying manner
8. collection
9. proved
10. glaring
11. inability; failing
12. toyed or played with
13. searched
14. swearing
15. useless
16. in a holy manner

A=7	B=11	C=6	D=10
E=14	F=2	G=15	H=3
I=12	J=8	K=9	L=5
M=1	N=13	O=4	P=16

Great Gilly Hopkins Vocabulary Magic Squares 3

Match the definition with the vocabulary word. Put your answers in the magic squares below. When your answers are correct, all columns and rows will add to the same number.

A. ELABORATELY
B. TENTATIVELY
C. FRACAS
D. DIVERTED
E. WOEFULLY
F. AUDIBLE
G. IRRITABILITY
H. SUBMISSION
I. ANOINTED
J. BELLIGERENTLY
K. PSYCHOLOGISTS
L. FUTILE
M. OBLIGINGLY
N. LADEN
O. KALEIDOSCOPIC
P. FLIRTATION

1. loaded down
2. testiness
3. useless
4. with great detail
5. therapists
6. with uncertainty
7. in an obeying manner
8. meekness; surrender
9. sadly
10. teasing
11. uproar
12. with hosility
13. changed; distracted
14. dedicated
15. hearable
16. brilliant

A=	B=	C=	D=
E=	F=	G=	H=
I=	J=	K=	L=
M=	N=	O=	P=

Great Gilly Hopkins Vocabulary Magic Squares 3 Answer Key

Match the definition with the vocabulary word. Put your answers in the magic squares below. When your answers are correct, all columns and rows will add to the same number.

A. ELABORATELY
B. TENTATIVELY
C. FRACAS
D. DIVERTED
E. WOEFULLY
F. AUDIBLE
G. IRRITABILITY
H. SUBMISSION
I. ANOINTED
J. BELLIGERENTLY
K. PSYCHOLOGISTS
L. FUTILE
M. OBLIGINGLY
N. LADEN
O. KALEIDOSCOPIC
P. FLIRTATION

1. loaded down
2. testiness
3. useless
4. with great detail
5. therapists
6. with uncertainty
7. in an obeying manner
8. meekness; surrender
9. sadly
10. teasing
11. uproar
12. with hosility
13. changed; distracted
14. dedicated
15. hearable
16. brilliant

A=4	B=6	C=11	D=13
E=9	F=15	G=2	H=8
I=14	J=12	K=5	L=3
M=7	N=1	O=16	P=10

Great Gilly Hopkins Vocabulary Magic Squares 4

Match the definition with the vocabulary word. Put your answers in the magic squares below. When your answers are correct, all columns and rows will add to the same number.

A. PERPETUAL
B. PIOUSLY
C. LADEN
D. HEFTING
E. MONOGRAMMED
F. FEEBLE
G. STRICKEN
H. APPALLING
I. FLIRTATION
J. ANOINTED
K. SELF-RIGHTEOUS
L. BENIGNLY
M. CONFIRMED
N. EMPHATICALLY
O. REPERTORY
P. VENGEANCE

1. in a holy manner
2. troubled
3. pure
4. intensely
5. proved
6. favorably
7. shocking
8. endless
9. revenge
10. teasing
11. designed with letters
12. lifting
13. loaded down
14. weak
15. dedicated
16. collection

A=	B=	C=	D=
E=	F=	G=	H=
I=	J=	K=	L=
M=	N=	O=	P=

Great Gilly Hopkins Vocabulary Magic Squares 4 Answer Key

Match the definition with the vocabulary word. Put your answers in the magic squares below. When your answers are correct, all columns and rows will add to the same number.

A. PERPETUAL
B. PIOUSLY
C. LADEN
D. HEFTING
E. MONOGRAMMED
F. FEEBLE
G. STRICKEN
H. APPALLING
I. FLIRTATION
J. ANOINTED
K. SELF-RIGHTEOUS
L. BENIGNLY
M. CONFIRMED
N. EMPHATICALLY
O. REPERTORY
P. VENGEANCE

1. in a holy manner
2. troubled
3. pure
4. intensely
5. proved
6. favorably
7. shocking
8. endless
9. revenge
10. teasing
11. designed with letters
12. lifting
13. loaded down
14. weak
15. dedicated
16. collection

A=8	B=1	C=13	D=12
E=11	F=14	G=2	H=7
I=10	J=15	K=3	L=6
M=5	N=4	O=16	P=9

Great Gilly Hopkins Vocabulary Word Search 1

E	N	T	H	R	A	L	L	E	D	G	D	E	M	T	N	Y	Y	D	B
M	I	M	B	E	C	I	L	E	C	E	S	K	J	O	Z	N	H	E	X
B	J	Z	W	J	Y	E	S	L	L	N	S	P	I	R	O	S	L	D	M
R	F	L	U	T	E	D	P	F	A	P	Q	T	G	G	X	L	R	E	B
A	H	W	F	R	V	R	I	P	X	B	I	U	A	P	I	C	L	L	K
C	Y	T	I	L	C	R	X	S	P	R	O	W	A	G	H	I	R	I	V
E	U	N	B	G	T	E	Q	C	A	L	R	R	E	V	T	P	L	N	H
J	G	L	C	C	A	N	O	P	I	E	D	R	I	U	E	J	N	Q	W
E	Y	F	I	H	F	R	P	Q	R	S	E	V	F	O	D	R	V	U	X
N	L	T	K	N	G	A	T	H	H	N	D	S	D	U	Q	I	E	P
G	B	A	G	Z	A	L	H	P	T	G	E	V	H	R	D	S	G	N	Q
U	A	P	Y	G	L	R	S	L	X	B	L	Y	R	G	H	T	L	C	G
L	R	P	L	N	M	L	Y	T	I	N	E	C	S	B	O	Z	V	Y	S
F	O	A	L	I	G	T	K	J	N	N	C	N	M	D	Q	D	L	G	C
E	X	L	U	T	D	D	R	O	G	R	T	A	I	T	S	S	W	S	D
D	E	L	F	F	I	R	I	R	Q	E	A	L	N	G	U	K	T	A	R
E	N	I	E	E	C	T	A	V	L	P	B	C	A	O	N	R	X	L	J
H	I	N	O	H	A	V	E	B	E	E	L	F	I	D	I	L	P	V	G
T	P	G	W	T	E	L	E	S	M	R	E	P	R	C	E	N	Y	A	Q
E	P	Q	R	D	B	E	V	L	J	T	T	Z	K	A	D	N	T	G	D
E	L	I	C	I	F	V	G	H	R	O	K	E	X	R	C	Z	T	E	W
S	L	D	D	K	V	T	M	W	V	R	N	S	D	Q	P	A	N	G	D
F	S	U	O	M	Y	N	O	N	A	Y	G	A	U	D	I	E	S	T	K
F	A	N	A	T	I	C	B	A	R	R	A	C	U	D	A	T	D	C	J

changed; distracted (8)
collection (9)
concerning cooking (8)
decoratively covered between the tops of bedposts (8)
dedicated (8)
delicious (10)
fascinated (10)
favorably (8)
flashiest (8)
flooded (8)
ghost (10)
glaring (7)
having grooves (6)
hearable (7)
hug (7)
impressed deeply (8)
in a holy manner (7)
lifting (7)
loaded down (5)
maniac (7)
misery (5)
moron; dimwit (8)
neglect;wrongdoing (11)
predatory fish (9)
raged; fumed (7)
rescue; save (7)
sadly (8)
searched (7)
shocking (9)
stretch (7)
swearing (9)
teasing (10)
toyed or played with (7)
trembling (9)
troubled (8)
unable to stop (10)
unsigned (9)
uproar (6)
useless (6)
weak (6)
with great difficulty (11)
with hosility (13)

Great Gilly Hopkins Vocabulary Word Search 1 Answer Key

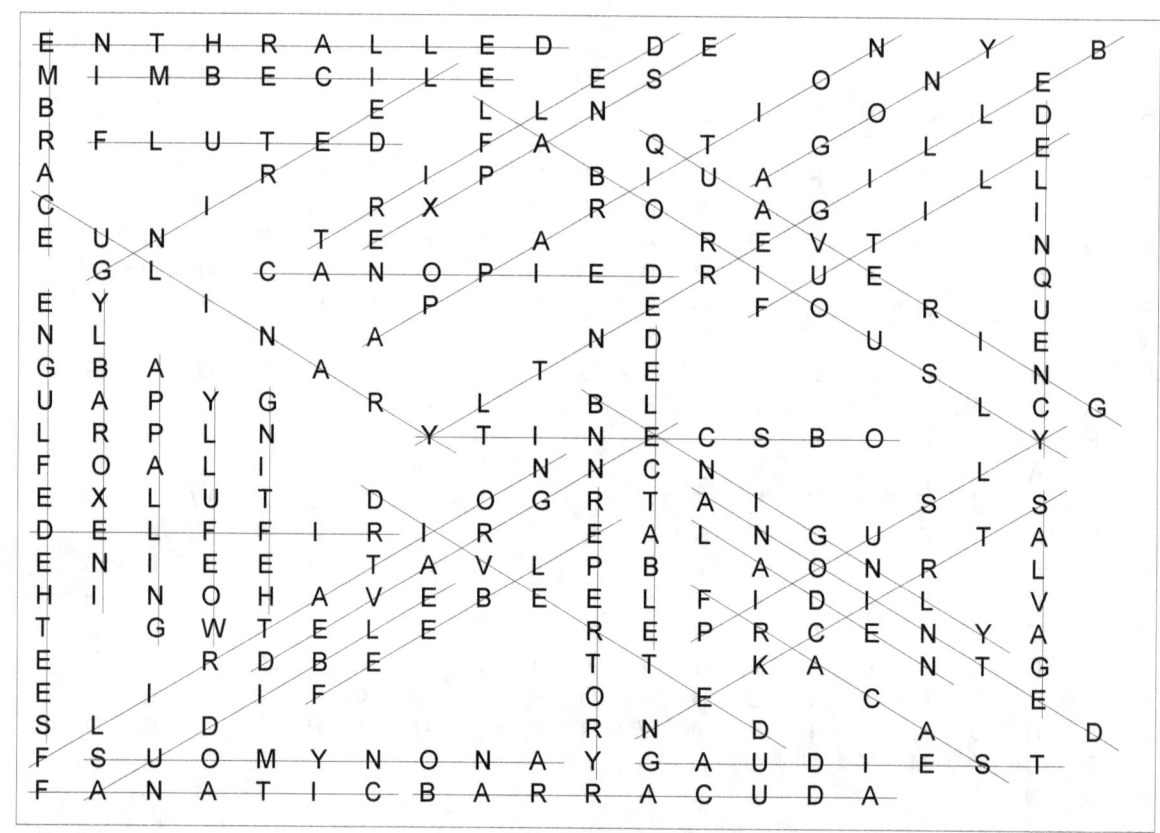

changed; distracted (8)
collection (9)
concerning cooking (8)
decoratively covered between the tops of bedposts (8)
dedicated (8)
delicious (10)
fascinated (10)
favorably (8)
flashiest (8)
flooded (8)
ghost (10)
glaring (7)
having grooves (6)
hearable (7)
hug (7)
impressed deeply (8)
in a holy manner (7)
lifting (7)
loaded down (5)
maniac (7)
misery (5)
moron; dimwit (8)
neglect;wrongdoing (11)

predatory fish (9)
raged; fumed (7)
rescue; save (7)
sadly (8)
searched (7)
shocking (9)
stretch (7)
swearing (9)
teasing (10)
toyed or played with (7)
trembling (9)
troubled (8)
unable to stop (10)
unsigned (9)
uproar (6)
useless (6)
weak (6)
with great difficulty (11)
with hosility (13)

Great Gilly Hopkins Vocabulary Word Search 2

```
P E R P E T U A L M Y K X D T F R A S V
S T B D Y T I N E C S B O E Y R I P A K
I N A W I W O E F U L L Y L L A F P L H
R Y R L X V P S O D K G G L L C F A V V
R G R E V S E M T J Y N Y A H A L R A Q
I V A E P L Y R M R I K T R M S E I G X
T Z C R S N Y M T G I L X H A N D T E P
A C U I O T E H I E J C E T V G N I I Y
B G D N W V L P C D N K N X Q O O G X
I S A G R F B Y L N G I N E B Y U N P M
L R U U U O A Y G R N V C V N S I O Y Y
I E D T D L T W A E I A H T L T L I V S
T I I E C I C V C L R P N Y F R I S A J
Y L B N U F E F L B E T M E R N N S R Q
E E L G L D L S M E V S H R C O E I I M
F D E U I X E E T E A P Q O I R X M A Z
L N K L N M D C D F U D M T D E O B T D
U A B F A N B E M B Q P A E T P R U I T
T H F E R D T E T T E T I X S E A S O J
E C Y D Y N E P C T R P H P B R B M N F
D E L F I R T N E I O Q K A N T L X S J
S K J O L M G N L N L Y W N H O Y Z V H
F A N A T I C F A P X E Q S R R D H P Z
D A M N G E H C S E E T H E D Y Q Q W W
```

changed; distracted (8)
collection (9)
concerning cooking (8)
decoratively covered between the tops of bedposts (8)
dedicated (8)
delicious (10)
endless (9)
fascinated (10)
favorably (8)
flashiest (8)
flooded (8)
ghost (10)
glaring (7)
glass light hanging from the ceiling (10)
having grooves (6)
hearable (7)
hug (7)
impressed deeply (8)
in a holy manner (7)
in an obeying manner (10)
inability; failing (12)
lifting (7)
loaded down (5)

maniac (7)
meekness; surrender (10)
misery (5)
moron; dimwit (8)
predatory fish (9)
raged; fumed (7)
rescue; save (7)
sadly (8)
searched (7)
stretch (7)
swearing (9)
teasing (10)
testiness (12)
toyed or played with (7)
trembling (9)
troubled (8)
unable to stop (10)
unsigned (9)
uproar (6)
useless (6)
variety (10)
weak (6)

Great Gilly Hopkins Vocabulary Word Search 2 Answer Key

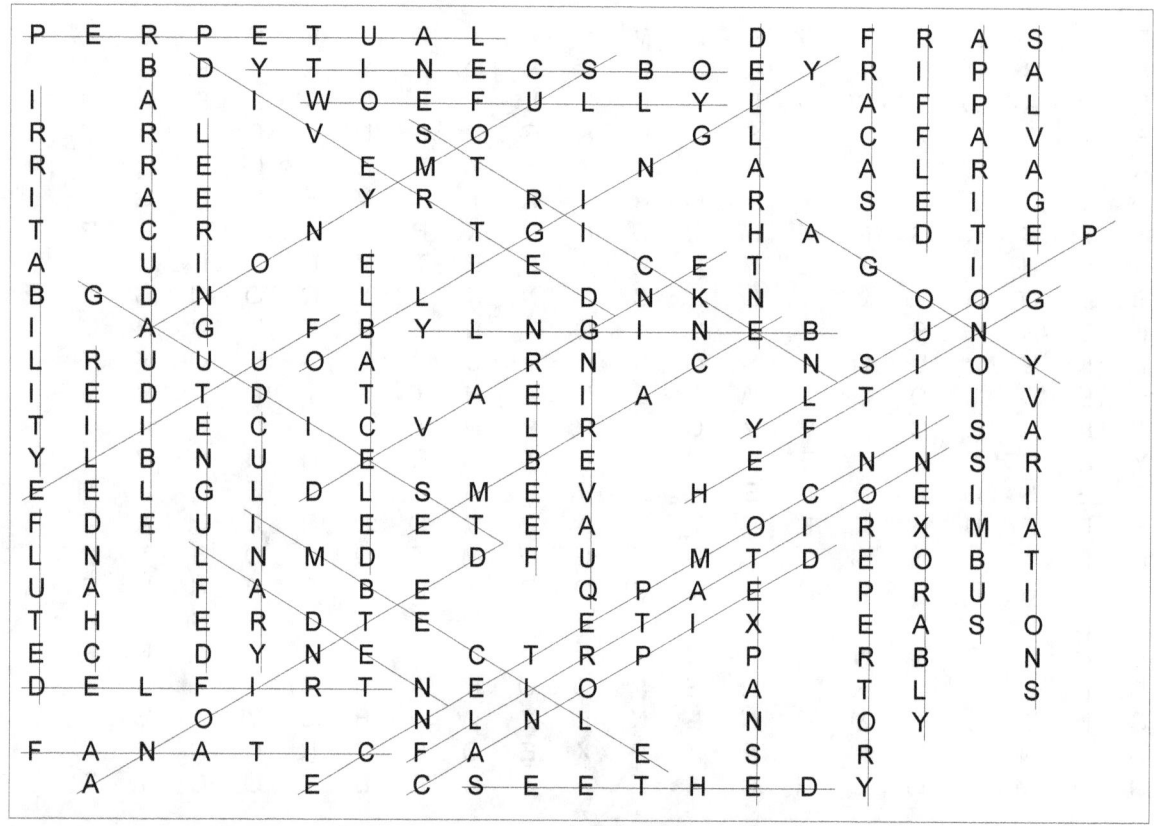

changed; distracted (8)
collection (9)
concerning cooking (8)
decoratively covered between the tops of bedposts (8)
dedicated (8)
delicious (10)
endless (9)
fascinated (10)
favorably (8)
flashiest (8)
flooded (8)
ghost (10)
glaring (7)
glass light hanging from the ceiling (10)
having grooves (6)
hearable (7)
hug (7)
impressed deeply (8)
in a holy manner (7)
in an obeying manner (10)
inability; failing (12)
lifting (7)
loaded down (5)

maniac (7)
meekness; surrender (10)
misery (5)
moron; dimwit (8)
predatory fish (9)
raged; fumed (7)
rescue; save (7)
sadly (8)
searched (7)
stretch (7)
swearing (9)
teasing (10)
testiness (12)
toyed or played with (7)
trembling (9)
troubled (8)
unable to stop (10)
unsigned (9)
uproar (6)
useless (6)
variety (10)
weak (6)

Great Gilly Hopkins Vocabulary Word Search 3

```
A S A M P K W T R S C L X Y M W M C H B
U E G L K I D O T V C F L S L W A G E F
D L O D W E O R E V L E W P A N S K F P
I F N S L D I U L F V E N Y O L S B T S
B - Y F G C B W S I U B S P M K V C I X
L R F L K K V C T L V L I F F H Q A N Z
E I N E X O R A B L Y E L E E R I N G V
R G N C L L T N R F D I N Y M P A N S E
C H L A G N N O H I R E N G S B I C L C
H T D V E M Q I K T A D N E E R R H A D
A E E T Q M J N A O E T E G E A E A E S
N O M W C K J T L R B T I V R L N M C V
D U R P L R I E E A H S A O I A M C T E
E S I J H O Q D I E N U C C N A V Y E R
L M F L N A I X D S Q O E E R S R E Q B
I W N M T O T H O W U B N G N A R K D Y
E M O B R P L I S X M B O Y N I F M F K
R X C B A K E N C I E N M I M C T E U J
Z M M D Q R S R O A O X L I I O N Y T R
Y E W B D S R F P M L U P T S G U M I D
T R I F L E D A I E C L A A U S Q S L X
W F L U T E D D C W T N Y L N G I N E B
G A U D I E S T X U A U F N Y S Z O Y R
R E P E R T O R Y F D E A T Q X E Z N D
A P P A L L I N G M D A V L Y Q Q S B J
```

AGONY	EMBROIDERED	HEFTING	RIFFLED
ANOINTED	EMPHATICALLY	IMBECILE	SALVAGE
ANONYMOUS	ENGRAVED	INEXORABLY	SEETHED
APPALLING	ENGULFED	KALEIDOSCOPIC	SELF-RIGHTEOUS
AUDIBLE	EXPANSE	LADEN	STRICKEN
BARRACUDA	FANATIC	LEERING	SUBMISSION
BENIGNLY	FEEBLE	MONOGRAMMED	TENTATIVELY
CANOPIED	FLIRTATION	OBSCENITY	TRIFLED
CHANDELIER	FLUTED	PERPETUAL	VARIATIONS
CONFIRMED	FRACAS	PIOUSLY	VENGEANCE
CULINARY	FUTILE	QUAVERING	WOEFULLY
EMBRACE	GAUDIEST	REPERTORY	

Great Gilly Hopkins Vocabulary Word Search 3 Answer Key

AGONY	EMBROIDERED	HEFTING	RIFFLED
ANOINTED	EMPHATICALLY	IMBECILE	SALVAGE
ANONYMOUS	ENGRAVED	INEXORABLY	SEETHED
APPALLING	ENGULFED	KALEIDOSCOPIC	SELF-RIGHTEOUS
AUDIBLE	EXPANSE	LADEN	STRICKEN
BARRACUDA	FANATIC	LEERING	SUBMISSION
BENIGNLY	FEEBLE	MONOGRAMMED	TENTATIVELY
CANOPIED	FLIRTATION	OBSCENITY	TRIFLED
CHANDELIER	FLUTED	PERPETUAL	VARIATIONS
CONFIRMED	FRACAS	PIOUSLY	VENGEANCE
CULINARY	FUTILE	QUAVERING	WOEFULLY
EMBRACE	GAUDIEST	REPERTORY	

Great Gilly Hopkins Vocabulary Word Search 4

```
J Q P M N D E L E C T A B L E D J B Q V
A D J N E S U B M I S S I O N I H E G L
U N C J D A D U C A R R A B W V H N N P
D N S U A E R E P T O R Y E I I I J
I M R E L E N T L E S S L Y N R X G R Q
B V R B L I R V S I T D Z J E T F N E R
L L E I I N Y E R N N H E B E A L V R
E E T F F R L A I N T Q L E E D N Y A R
F U C L L R C R S G A U C F O A C U Q
F P E A U U K I E Y B E A E I T T Q H
S D E F N E T I T O E R A T N B I E X B
F E E R N O D E R A B X A N Y C C N K C
C O E X P U P I D M B T P L C N Y T G G
W S A T A E O I E F R I L A E E K A I Z
K Z N G H U T T E I P A L T N P T T M D
W G O Y S E C U L D C D E I D S D I B K
M N N L Z M D F A I E P M E T E E V E X
Y I Y B H V R T T L M D M X F Y L E C Y
N L M A S B R A F O E R E L J Y L L I J
F L O R Z B B H F C V I G U S L F A Y L H
P A U O L P I N A F A G D S M R R V E M
N P S X M R I R N V N P U D M A H B Z P
H P Q E G M G O L E B O S F Q C T G H Q
S A R N S N C A N O I N T E D A N Q V F
L F K I E X S D R P N S L H Q S E Y M S
```

AGONY	DIVERTED	FUTILE	QUAVERING
ANOINTED	EMBRACE	GAUDIEST	RELENTLESSLY
ANONYMOUS	EMPHATICALLY	HEFTING	REPERTORY
APPALLING	ENGRAVED	IMBECILE	RIFFLED
AUDIBLE	ENGULFED	INCOMPETENCE	SALVAGE
BARRACUDA	ENTHRALLED	INEXORABLY	SEETHED
BENIGNLY	EXPANSE	IRRITABILITY	STRICKEN
CANOPIED	FANATIC	LABORIOUSLY	SUBMISSION
CONFIRMED	FEEBLE	LADEN	TENTATIVELY
CULINARY	FLIRTATION	LEERING	TRIFLED
DELECTABLE	FLUTED	PERPETUAL	VENGEANCE
DELINQUENCY	FRACAS	PIOUSLY	WOEFULLY

Great Gilly Hopkins Vocabulary Word Search 4 Answer Key

AGONY	DIVERTED	FUTILE	QUAVERING
ANOINTED	EMBRACE	GAUDIEST	RELENTLESSLY
ANONYMOUS	EMPHATICALLY	HEFTING	REPERTORY
APPALLING	ENGRAVED	IMBECILE	RIFFLED
AUDIBLE	ENGULFED	INCOMPETENCE	SALVAGE
BARRACUDA	ENTHRALLED	INEXORABLY	SEETHED
BENIGNLY	EXPANSE	IRRITABILITY	STRICKEN
CANOPIED	FANATIC	LABORIOUSLY	SUBMISSION
CONFIRMED	FEEBLE	LADEN	TENTATIVELY
CULINARY	FLIRTATION	LEERING	TRIFLED
DELECTABLE	FLUTED	PERPETUAL	VENGEANCE
DELINQUENCY	FRACAS	PIOUSLY	WOEFULLY

Great Gilly Hopkins Vocabulary Crossword 1

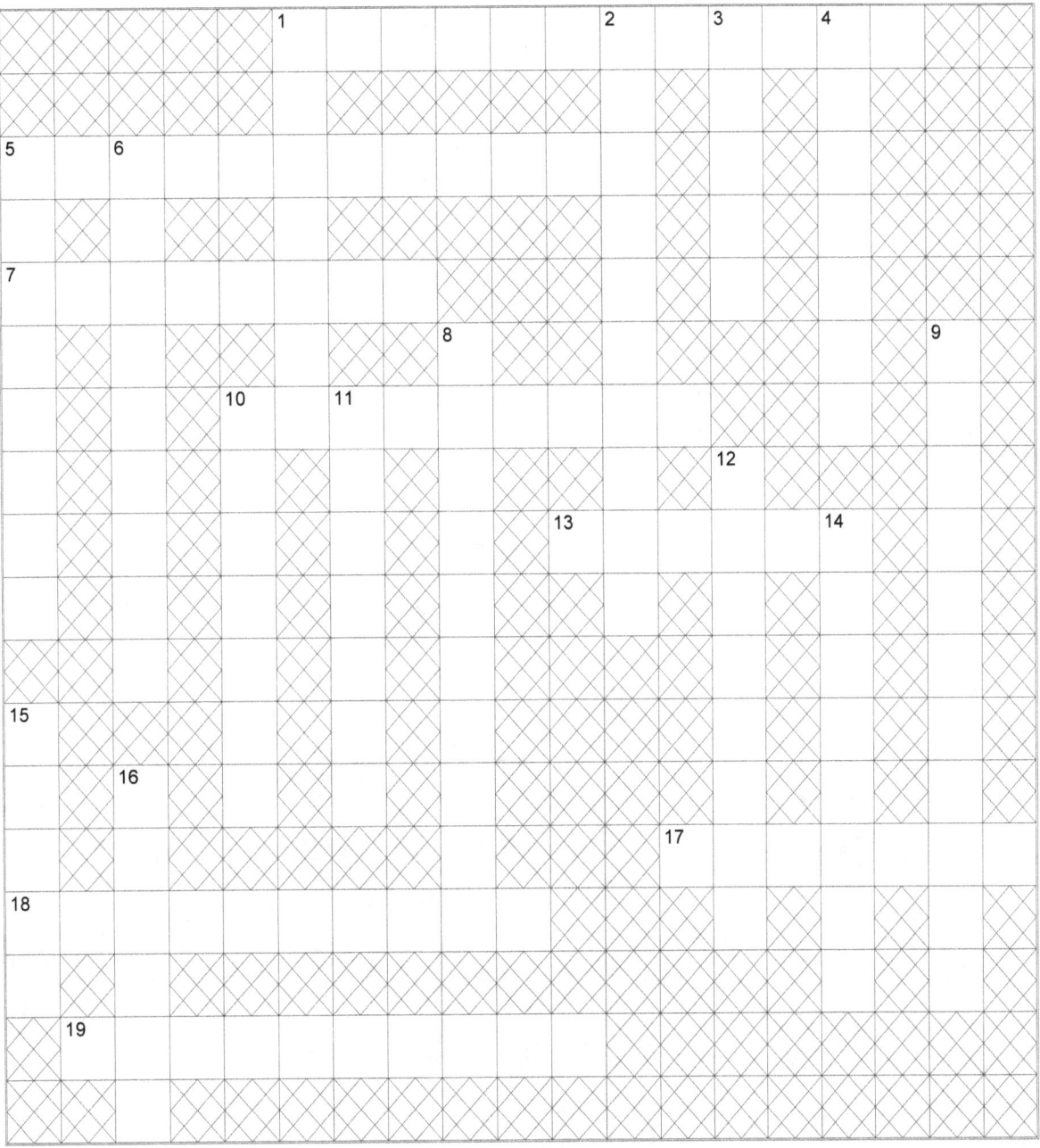

Across
1. intensely
5. inability; failing
7. favorably
10. endless
13. having grooves
17. raged; fumed
18. fascinated
19. teasing

Down
1. stretch
2. unable to stop
3. misery
4. glaring
5. moron; dimwit
6. proved
8. delicious
9. with great detail
10. in a holy manner
11. searched
12. troubled
14. changed; distracted
15. loaded down
16. useless

Great Gilly Hopkins Vocabulary Crossword 1 Answer Key

Across
1. intensely
5. inability; failing
7. favorably
10. endless
13. having grooves
17. raged; fumed
18. fascinated
19. teasing

Down
1. stretch
2. unable to stop
3. misery
4. glaring
5. moron; dimwit
6. proved
8. delicious
9. with great detail
10. in a holy manner
11. searched
12. troubled
14. changed; distracted
15. loaded down
16. useless

Great Gilly Hopkins Vocabulary Crossword 2

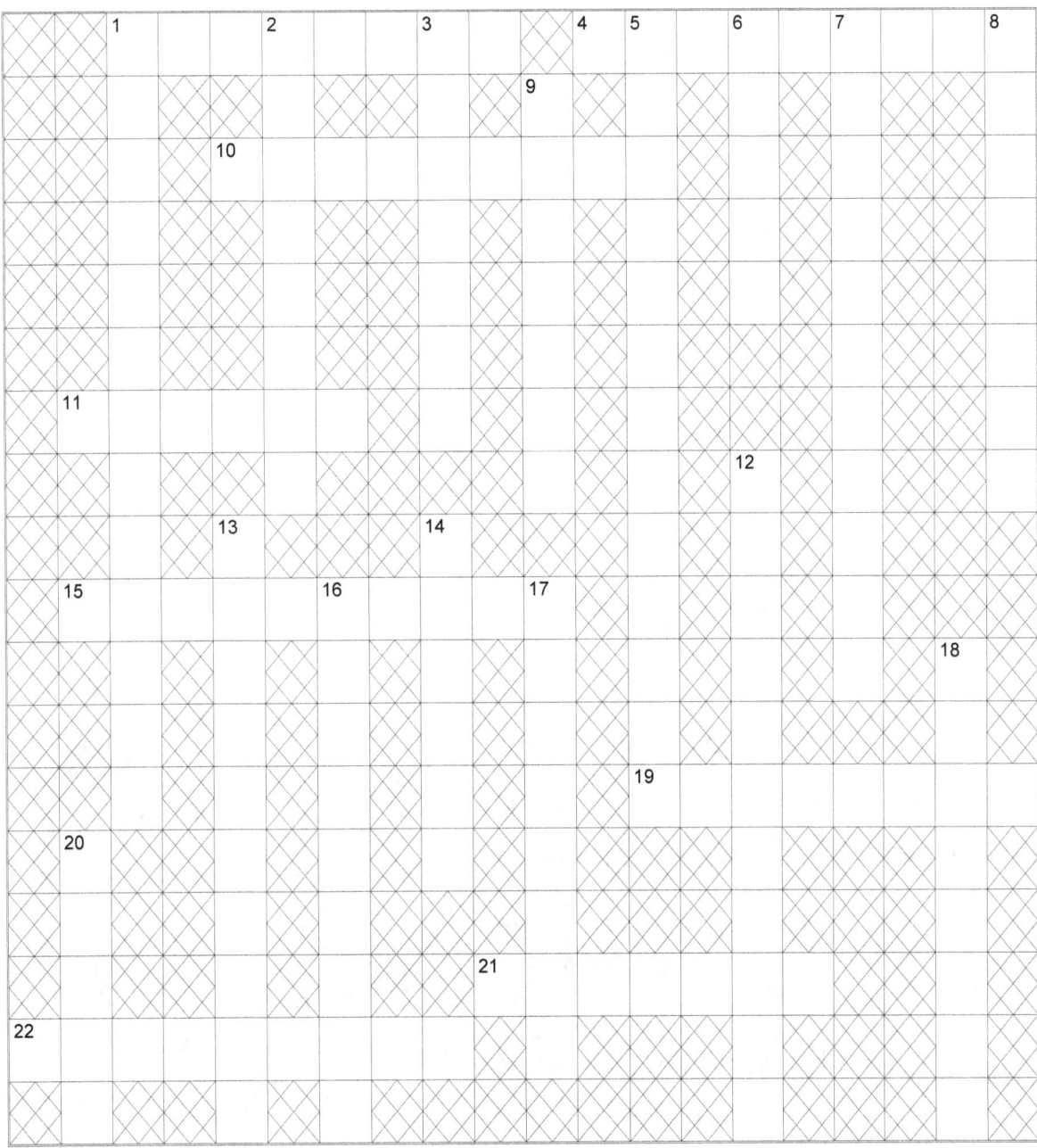

Across
1. favorably
4. shocking
10. swearing
11. weak
15. fascinated
19. troubled
21. raged; fumed
22. endless

Down
1. with hosility
2. moron; dimwit
3. glaring
5. therapists
6. misery
7. with great difficulty
8. flashiest
9. searched
12. with great detail
13. glass light hanging from the ceiling
14. having grooves
16. unsigned
17. changed; distracted
18. sadly
20. loaded down

Great Gilly Hopkins Vocabulary Crossword 2 Answer Key

	1 B	E	2 N	I	3 G	N	4 Y		4 A	5 P	P	6 A	7 L	L	I	N	8 G
	E		M		E			9 R		S		G	A				A
	L		10 O	B	S	C	E	N	I	T	Y		O		B			U
	L		E		R		F		C			N		O			D
	I		C		I		F		H			Y		R			I
	G		I		N		L		O				I			E
11 F	E	E	B	L	E		G		E		L			O		S
	R		E				D		O		12 E		U			T
	E		13 C		14 F				G		L		S			
15 E	N	T	H	R	A	L	L	E	17 D		I		A		L		
	T		A		N		U		I		S		B		Y		18 W
	L		N		O		T		V		T		O				O
	Y		D		N		E		E		19 S	T	R	I	C	K	E	N
20 L			E		Y		D		R			A				F
A			L		M				T			T				U
D			I		O		21 S	E	E	T	H	E	D			L
22 P	E	R	P	E	T	U	A	L		D			L			L
N				R		S						Y			Y

Across
1. favorably
4. shocking
10. swearing
11. weak
15. fascinated
19. troubled
21. raged; fumed
22. endless

Down
1. with hosility
2. moron; dimwit
3. glaring
5. therapists
6. misery
7. with great difficulty
8. flashiest
9. searched
12. with great detail
13. glass light hanging from the ceiling
14. having grooves
16. unsigned
17. changed; distracted
18. sadly
20. loaded down

Great Gilly Hopkins Vocabulary Crossword 3

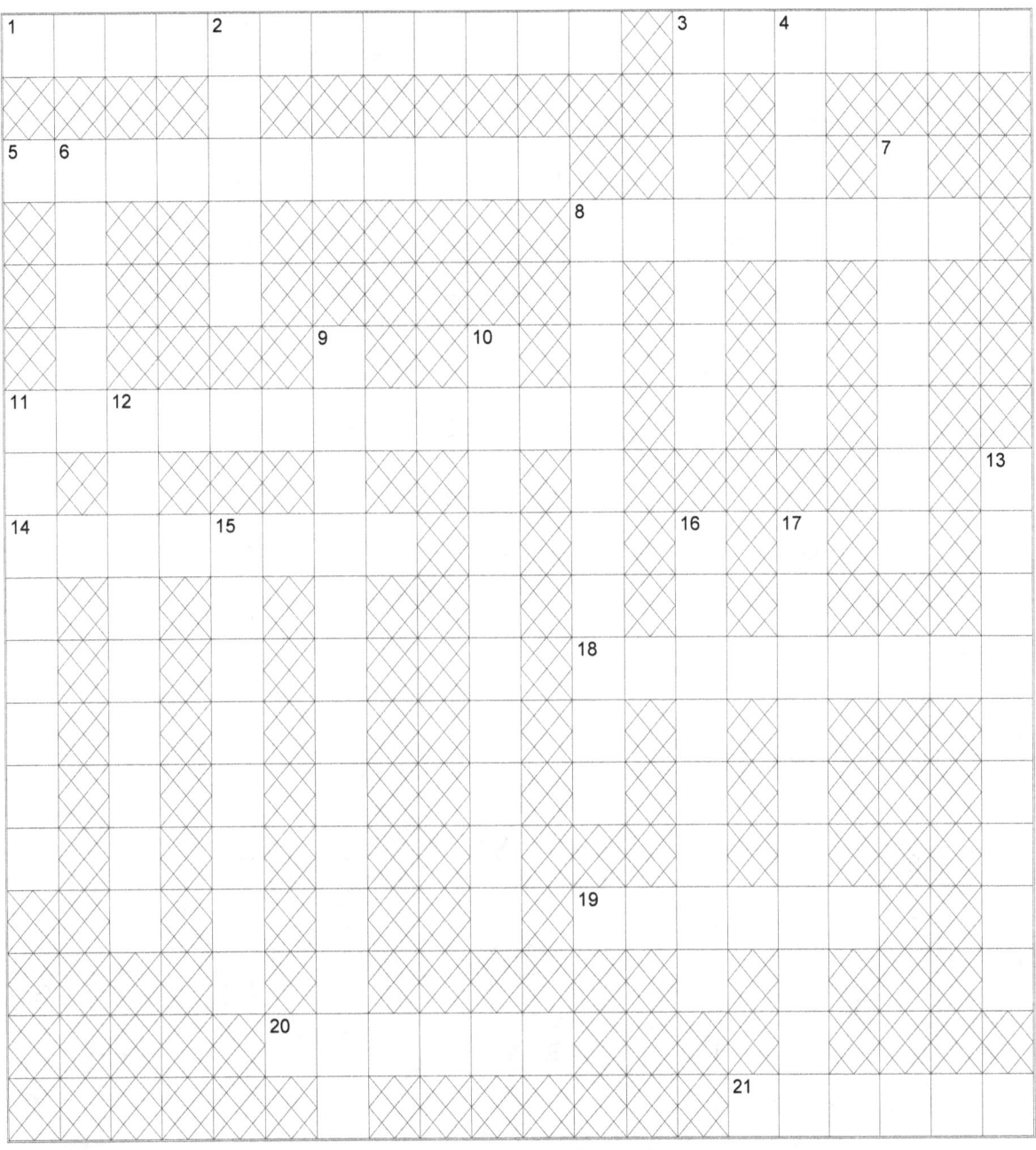

Across
1. intensely
3. raged; fumed
5. with great detail
8. changed; distracted
11. inability; failing
14. favorably
18. predatory fish
19. weak
20. having grooves
21. uproar

Down
2. misery
3. rescue; save
4. hug
6. loaded down
7. glaring
8. delicious
9. with hosility
10. fascinated
11. moron; dimwit
12. proved
13. shocking
15. flashiest
16. troubled
17. glass light hanging from the ceiling

Great Gilly Hopkins Vocabulary Crossword 3 Answer Key

	1 E	M	2 P A G	H	A	T	I	C	A	L	L	Y		3 S A L E	4 E M B	T	H	E	D

Across:
- 1. EMPHATICALLY
- 3. SEETHED
- 5. ELABORATELY
- 8. DIVERTED
- 11. INCOMPETENCE
- 14. BENIGNLY
- 18. BARRACUDA
- 19. FEEBLE
- 20. FLUTED
- 21. FRACAS

Down:
- 2. AGONY
- 4. EMBRACE
- 6. LABORED
- 7. LIGHT (LBD...)
- 8. DELEGATE
- 9. BELLIGERENTLY
- 10. ELECTRIFIED
- 11. IMBECILE
- 12. CONFIRMED
- 13. APPALLING
- 15. GIGANTIC (?)
- 16. STAT...
- 17. CHANDELIER

Across
1. intensely
3. raged; fumed
5. with great detail
8. changed; distracted
11. inability; failing
14. favorably
18. predatory fish
19. weak
20. having grooves
21. uproar

Down
2. misery
3. rescue; save
4. hug
6. loaded down
7. glaring
8. delicious
9. with hosility
10. fascinated
11. moron; dimwit
12. proved
13. shocking
15. flashiest
16. troubled
17. glass light hanging from the ceiling

Great Gilly Hopkins Vocabulary Crossword 4

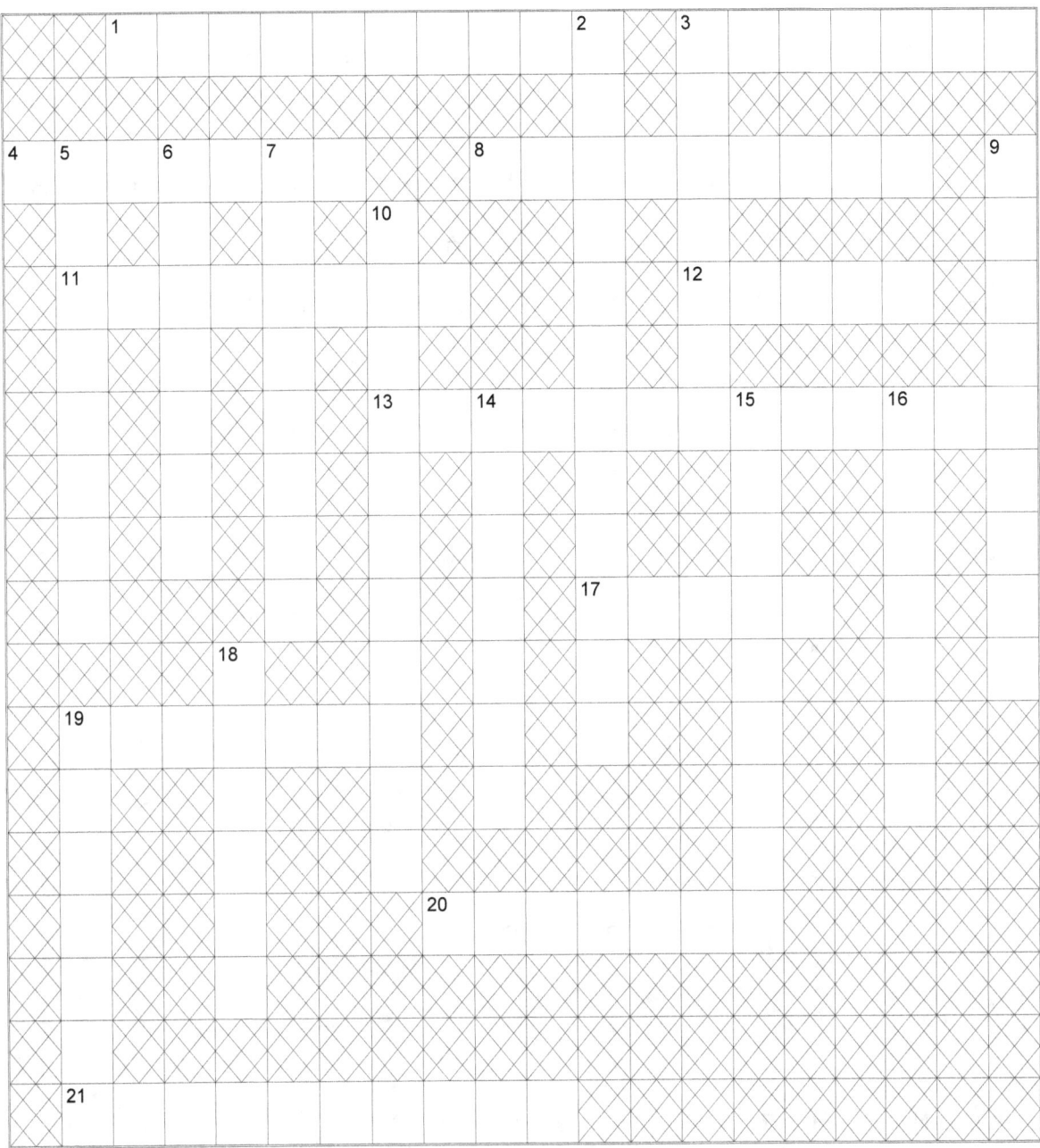

Across
1. delicious
3. raged; fumed
4. searched
8. shocking
11. favorably
12. misery
13. with hosility
17. loaded down
19. hug
20. in a holy manner
21. fascinated

Down
2. intensely
3. rescue; save
5. moron; dimwit
6. maniac
7. impressed deeply
9. unsigned
10. with great detail
14. glaring
15. collection
16. toyed or played with
18. uproar
19. stretch

Great Gilly Hopkins Vocabulary Crossword 4 Answer Key

		¹D	E	L	E	C	T	A	B	L	²E		³S	E	E	T	H	E	D	
											M		A							
⁴R	⁵I	⁶F	⁷F	L	E	D		⁸A	P	P	A	L	L	I	N	G				⁹A
	M	A		N			¹⁰E				H		V							N
	¹¹B	E	N	I	G	N	L	Y			A		¹²A	G	O	N	Y			O
	E			A			A				T		G							N
	¹³C			A		¹³B	¹⁴E	L	L	I	G	E	¹⁵R	E	N	¹⁶T	L	Y	
	I			V			O		E		C		E				R		M	
	L			C			E		R		A		P				I		O	
	E			D			A		R		¹⁷L	A	D	E	N		F		U	
			¹⁸F				T		I		L		R				L		S	
	¹⁹E	M	B	R	A	C	E		N		Y		T				E			
	X			A			L		G				O				D			
	P			C			Y						R							
	A			A			²⁰P	I	O	U	S	L	Y							
	N			S																
	S																			
	²¹E	N	T	H	R	A	L	L	E	D										

Across
1. delicious
3. raged; fumed
4. searched
8. shocking
11. favorably
12. misery
13. with hosility
17. loaded down
19. hug
20. in a holy manner
21. fascinated

Down
2. intensely
3. rescue; save
5. moron; dimwit
6. maniac
7. impressed deeply
9. unsigned
10. with great detail
14. glaring
15. collection
16. toyed or played with
18. uproar
19. stretch

Great Gilly Hopkins Vocabulary Juggle Letters 1

1. CNIEOBSTY = 1. _____
   swearing

2. LUPREAPET = 2. _____
   endless

3. ITOVARANSI = 3. _____
   variety

4. IEEGLNR = 4. _____
   glaring

5. VETDIRDE = 5. _____
   changed; distracted

6. SIIDEOKPLAOCC = 6. _____
   brilliant

7. TSKIECNR = 7. _____
   troubled

8. AIIRLTITBIYR = 8. _____
   testiness

9. NDEQNLCYEIU = 9. _____
   neglect; wrongdoing

10. BOIYILGNGL = 10. _____
    in an obeying manner

11. RSAAFC = 11. _____
    uproar

12. NVAECNEGE = 12. _____
    revenge

13. NOGYA = 13. _____
    misery

14. RTEOLEABALY = 14. _____
    with great detail

15. TALRDLENEH = 15. _____
    fascinated

Great Gilly Hopkins Vocabulary Juggle Letters 1 Answer Key

1. CNIEOBSTY = 1. OBSCENITY
   swearing
2. LUPREAPET = 2. PERPETUAL
   endless
3. ITOVARANSI = 3. VARIATIONS
   variety
4. IEEGLNR = 4. LEERING
   glaring
5. VETDIRDE = 5. DIVERTED
   changed; distracted
6. SIIDEOKPLAOCC = 6. KALEIDOSCOPIC
   brilliant
7. TSKIECNR = 7. STRICKEN
   troubled
8. AIIRLTITBIYR = 8. IRRITABILITY
   testiness
9. NDEQNLCYEIU = 9. DELINQUENCY
   neglect; wrongdoing
10. BOIYILGNGL = 10. OBLIGINGLY
    in an obeying manner
11. RSAAFC = 11. FRACAS
    uproar
12. NVAECNEGE = 12. VENGEANCE
    revenge
13. NOGYA = 13. AGONY
    misery
14. RTEOLEABALY = 14. ELABORATELY
    with great detail
15. TALRDLENEH = 15. ENTHRALLED
    fascinated

Great Gilly Hopkins Vocabulary Juggle Letters 2

1. TEENLSELSRLY = 1. _____
   steadily
2. LAIUEBD = 2. _____
   hearable
3. YEIUNQDLECN = 3. _____
   neglect;wrongdoing
4. GCOSOHSPTSYIL = 4. _____
   therapists
5. OEDINCPA = 5. _____
   decoratively covered between the tops of bedposts
6. SBNTYCIOE = 6. _____
   swearing
7. XANPSEE = 7. _____
   stretch
8. HLLTEEADRN = 8. _____
   fascinated
9. IPLAGANPL = 9. _____
   shocking
10. UONNOSYAM = 10. _____
    unsigned
11. UEWLFYOL = 11. _____
    sadly
12. EEBLCATDLE = 12. _____
    delicious
13. HEDAIECRLN = 13. _____
    glass light hanging from the ceiling
14. RODIMEFCN = 14. _____
    proved
15. DEHEETS = 15. _____
    raged; fumed

Great Gilly Hopkins Vocabulary Juggle Letters 2 Answer Key

1. TEENLSELSRLY = 1. RELENTLESSLY
   steadily

2. LAIUEBD = 2. AUDIBLE
   hearable

3. YEIUNQDLECN = 3. DELINQUENCY
   neglect; wrongdoing

4. GCOSOHSPTSYIL = 4. PSYCHOLOGISTS
   therapists

5. OEDINCPA = 5. CANOPIED
   decoratively covered between the tops of bedposts

6. SBNTYCIOE = 6. OBSCENITY
   swearing

7. XANPSEE = 7. EXPANSE
   stretch

8. HLLTEEADRN = 8. ENTHRALLED
   fascinated

9. IPLAGANPL = 9. APPALLING
   shocking

10. UONNOSYAM = 10. ANONYMOUS
    unsigned

11. UEWLFYOL = 11. WOEFULLY
    sadly

12. EEBLCATDLE = 12. DELECTABLE
    delicious

13. HEDAIECRLN = 13. CHANDELIER
    glass light hanging from the ceiling

14. RODIMEFCN = 14. CONFIRMED
    proved

15. DEHEETS = 15. SEETHED
    raged; fumed

Great Gilly Hopkins Vocabulary Juggle Letters 3

1. TTLNORFAII = 1. _____
   teasing

2. LVAGASE = 2. _____
   rescue; save

3. ENITGHF = 3. _____
   lifting

4. NSLTSELEYERL = 4. _____
   steadily

5. RTNDAEELLH = 5. _____
   fascinated

6. BYOUIAROSLL = 6. _____
   with great difficulty

7. DTHSEEE = 7. _____
   raged; fumed

8. ETRVDDIE = 8. _____
   changed; distracted

9. LRTIDFE = 9. _____
   toyed or played with

10. IOODPIACKCESL =10. _____
    brilliant

11. ENTNIOPECCME =11. _____
    inability; failing

12. YBOAELARTEL =12. _____
    with great detail

13. NYLGGIIBOL =13. _____
    in an obeying manner

14. ILOUYPS =14. _____
    in a holy manner

15. CATINAF =15. _____
    maniac

Great Gilly Hopkins Vocabulary Juggle Letters 3 Answer Key

1. TTLNORFAII = 1. FLIRTATION
   teasing
2. LVAGASE = 2. SALVAGE
   rescue; save
3. ENITGHF = 3. HEFTING
   lifting
4. NSLTSELEYERL = 4. RELENTLESSLY
   steadily
5. RTNDAEELLH = 5. ENTHRALLED
   fascinated
6. BYOUIAROSLL = 6. LABORIOUSLY
   with great difficulty
7. DTHSEEE = 7. SEETHED
   raged; fumed
8. ETRVDDIE = 8. DIVERTED
   changed; distracted
9. LRTIDFE = 9. TRIFLED
   toyed or played with
10. IOODPIACKCESL = 10. KALEIDOSCOPIC
    brilliant
11. ENTNIOPECCME = 11. INCOMPETENCE
    inability; failing
12. YBOAELARTEL = 12. ELABORATELY
    with great detail
13. NYLGGIIBOL = 13. OBLIGINGLY
    in an obeying manner
14. ILOUYPS = 14. PIOUSLY
    in a holy manner
15. CATINAF = 15. FANATIC
    maniac

Great Gilly Hopkins Vocabulary Juggle Letters 4

1. UFHSIELSOTR-GE = 1. _____
   pure

2. EHEEDTS = 2. _____
   raged; fumed

3. OMNGARMEDOM = 3. _____
   designed with letters

4. YAOSONMNU = 4. _____
   unsigned

5. RNOFAITLIT = 5. _____
   teasing

6. DLNEA = 6. _____
   loaded down

7. CBAERME = 7. _____
   hug

8. ITNODEAN = 8. _____
   dedicated

9. NEIFRODMC = 9. _____
   proved

10. STIGHLPYSCOOS = 10. _____
    therapists

11. TNFGIHE = 11. _____
    lifting

12. ANCFIAT = 12. _____
    maniac

13. IPPAONRTAI = 13. _____
    ghost

14. EILMEIBC = 14. _____
    moron; dimwit

15. CTNSEOBYI = 15. _____
    swearing

Great Gilly Hopkins Vocabulary Juggle Letters 4 Answer Key

1. UFHSIELSOTR-GE = 1. SELF-RIGHTEOUS
   pure
2. EHEEDTS = 2. SEETHED
   raged; fumed
3. OMNGARMEDOM = 3. MONOGRAMMED
   designed with letters
4. YAOSONMNU = 4. ANONYMOUS
   unsigned
5. RNOFAITLIT = 5. FLIRTATION
   teasing
6. DLNEA = 6. LADEN
   loaded down
7. CBAERME = 7. EMBRACE
   hug
8. ITNODEAN = 8. ANOINTED
   dedicated
9. NEIFRODMC = 9. CONFIRMED
   proved
10. STIGHLPYSCOOS = 10. PSYCHOLOGISTS
    therapists
11. TNFGIHE = 11. HEFTING
    lifting
12. ANCFIAT = 12. FANATIC
    maniac
13. IPPAONRTAI = 13. APPARITION
    ghost
14. EILMEIBC = 14. IMBECILE
    moron; dimwit
15. CTNSEOBYI = 15. OBSCENITY
    swearing

AGONY	misery
ANOINTED	dedicated
ANONYMOUS	unsigned
APPALLING	shocking
APPARITION	ghost
AUDIBLE	hearable

BARRACUDA	predatory fish
BELLIGERENTLY	with hosility
BENIGNLY	favorably
CANOPIED	decoratively covered between the tops of bedposts
CHANDELIER	glass light hanging from the ceiling
CONFIRMED	proved

CULINARY	concerning cooking
DELECTABLE	delicious
DELINQUENCY	neglect; wrongdoing
DIVERTED	changed; distracted
ELABORATELY	with great detail
EMBRACE	hug

EMBROIDERED	having needlework
EMPHATICALLY	intensely
ENGRAVED	impressed deeply
ENGULFED	flooded
ENTHRALLED	fascinated
EXPANSE	stretch

FANATIC	maniac
FEEBLE	weak
FLIRTATION	teasing
FLUTED	having grooves
FRACAS	uproar
FUTILE	useless

GAUDIEST	flashiest
HEFTING	lifting
IMBECILE	moron; dimwit
INCOMPETENCE	inability; failing
INEXORABLY	unable to stop
IRRITABILITY	testiness

KALEIDOSCOPIC	brilliant
LABORIOUSLY	with great difficulty
LADEN	loaded down
LEERING	glaring
MONOGRAMMED	designed with letters
OBLIGINGLY	in an obeying manner

OBSCENITY	swearing
PERPETUAL	endless
PIOUSLY	in a holy manner
PSYCHOLOGISTS	therapists
QUAVERING	trembling
RELENTLESSLY	steadily

REPERTORY	collection
RIFFLED	searched
SALVAGE	rescue; save
SEETHED	raged; fumed
SELF-RIGHTEOUS	pure
STRICKEN	troubled

SUBMISSION	meekness; surrender
TENTATIVELY	with uncertainty
TRIFLED	toyed or played with
VARIATIONS	variety
VENGEANCE	revenge
WOEFULLY	sadly

Great Gilly Hopkins Vocabulary

CHANDELIER	EMPHATICALLY	OBSCENITY	IMBECILE	CULINARY
CANOPIED	EMBRACE	EMBROIDERED	FLUTED	BARRACUDA
DELECTABLE	DIVERTED	FREE SPACE	BENIGNLY	OBLIGINGLY
SEETHED	EXPANSE	TRIFLED	RELENTLESSLY	ENGRAVED
BELLIGERENTLY	LADEN	PSYCHOLOGISTS	VENGEANCE	AGONY

Great Gilly Hopkins Vocabulary

CONFIRMED	ENTHRALLED	APPARITION	TENTATIVELY	WOEFULLY
FANATIC	ANOINTED	FLIRTATION	ELABORATELY	SALVAGE
GAUDIEST	FEEBLE	FREE SPACE	IRRITABILITY	LABORIOUSLY
LEERING	INCOMPETENCE	DELINQUENCY	VARIATIONS	REPERTORY
MONOGRAMMED	ENGULFED	QUAVERING	APPALLING	HEFTING

Great Gilly Hopkins Vocabulary

MONOGRAMMED	BARRACUDA	STRICKEN	APPARITION	RIFFLED
IMBECILE	BELLIGERENTLY	QUAVERING	EXPANSE	APPALLING
EMBROIDERED	PSYCHOLOGISTS	FREE SPACE	DELECTABLE	CANOPIED
KALEIDOSCOPIC	OBSCENITY	TRIFLED	RELENTLESSLY	DELINQUENCY
PERPETUAL	DIVERTED	HEFTING	LABORIOUSLY	ANOINTED

Great Gilly Hopkins Vocabulary

PIOUSLY	ENGRAVED	LADEN	FUTILE	CULINARY
BENIGNLY	EMPHATICALLY	ENTHRALLED	AUDIBLE	AGONY
CHANDELIER	INCOMPETENCE	FREE SPACE	LEERING	EMBRACE
FLIRTATION	IRRITABILITY	ELABORATELY	VENGEANCE	SALVAGE
REPERTORY	CONFIRMED	GAUDIEST	SEETHED	SELF-RIGHTEOUS

Great Gilly Hopkins Vocabulary

SALVAGE	INCOMPETENCE	REPERTORY	DELINQUENCY	ENGULFED
FRACAS	TENTATIVELY	DIVERTED	OBSCENITY	KALEIDOSCOPIC
ENTHRALLED	ANOINTED	FREE SPACE	AGONY	FLUTED
APPARITION	SEETHED	CHANDELIER	IRRITABILITY	TRIFLED
APPALLING	STRICKEN	LEERING	DELECTABLE	EXPANSE

Great Gilly Hopkins Vocabulary

AUDIBLE	CANOPIED	CONFIRMED	VENGEANCE	RELENTLESSLY
RIFFLED	ENGRAVED	EMPHATICALLY	IMBECILE	CULINARY
ELABORATELY	BENIGNLY	FREE SPACE	EMBROIDERED	FANATIC
PERPETUAL	FLIRTATION	INEXORABLY	WOEFULLY	OBLIGINGLY
MONOGRAMMED	FUTILE	BARRACUDA	LABORIOUSLY	SELF-RIGHTEOUS

Great Gilly Hopkins Vocabulary

IRRITABILITY	OBSCENITY	ENTHRALLED	TENTATIVELY	BENIGNLY
AGONY	APPARITION	SUBMISSION	DELECTABLE	QUAVERING
ANONYMOUS	VARIATIONS	FREE SPACE	CANOPIED	SELF-RIGHTEOUS
PIOUSLY	FUTILE	BELLIGERENTLY	INCOMPETENCE	HEFTING
INEXORABLY	REPERTORY	RELENTLESSLY	ELABORATELY	DIVERTED

Great Gilly Hopkins Vocabulary

DELINQUENCY	EXPANSE	AUDIBLE	RIFFLED	EMBROIDERED
VENGEANCE	ENGRAVED	TRIFLED	EMPHATICALLY	PERPETUAL
ENGULFED	IMBECILE	FREE SPACE	LABORIOUSLY	GAUDIEST
LEERING	CULINARY	KALEIDOSCOPIC	APPALLING	PSYCHOLOGISTS
CONFIRMED	SALVAGE	EMBRACE	BARRACUDA	FLUTED

Great Gilly Hopkins Vocabulary

FUTILE	CHANDELIER	FRACAS	REPERTORY	EMBROIDERED
INEXORABLY	PERPETUAL	TRIFLED	DIVERTED	ENTHRALLED
EMBRACE	SUBMISSION	FREE SPACE	IMBECILE	STRICKEN
DELINQUENCY	MONOGRAMMED	CANOPIED	CONFIRMED	FLIRTATION
WOEFULLY	RIFFLED	SEETHED	GAUDIEST	TENTATIVELY

Great Gilly Hopkins Vocabulary

PIOUSLY	KALEIDOSCOPIC	DELECTABLE	ENGRAVED	BENIGNLY
EXPANSE	APPALLING	LEERING	CULINARY	LABORIOUSLY
QUAVERING	FANATIC	FREE SPACE	ANONYMOUS	AUDIBLE
BELLIGERENTLY	INCOMPETENCE	HEFTING	IRRITABILITY	SELF-RIGHTEOUS
SALVAGE	VENGEANCE	BARRACUDA	VARIATIONS	OBSCENITY

Great Gilly Hopkins Vocabulary

SELF-RIGHTEOUS	LEERING	EMBRACE	REPERTORY	MONOGRAMMED
ENTHRALLED	LADEN	QUAVERING	VENGEANCE	RIFFLED
EMPHATICALLY	BELLIGERENTLY	FREE SPACE	SUBMISSION	FEEBLE
BENIGNLY	HEFTING	ELABORATELY	CHANDELIER	TRIFLED
BARRACUDA	OBSCENITY	GAUDIEST	AUDIBLE	FLIRTATION

Great Gilly Hopkins Vocabulary

SEETHED	EXPANSE	ENGRAVED	OBLIGINGLY	FLUTED
PERPETUAL	ENGULFED	AGONY	FANATIC	APPALLING
INCOMPETENCE	CANOPIED	FREE SPACE	CONFIRMED	SALVAGE
STRICKEN	VARIATIONS	APPARITION	KALEIDOSCOPIC	RELENTLESSLY
PSYCHOLOGISTS	ANOINTED	EMBROIDERED	PIOUSLY	INEXORABLY

Great Gilly Hopkins Vocabulary

ENGULFED	QUAVERING	PERPETUAL	WOEFULLY	AGONY
EMBROIDERED	VARIATIONS	FRACAS	FUTILE	OBSCENITY
INCOMPETENCE	ENTHRALLED	FREE SPACE	FLIRTATION	IRRITABILITY
TENTATIVELY	PIOUSLY	BENIGNLY	APPALLING	RIFFLED
CANOPIED	IMBECILE	LABORIOUSLY	GAUDIEST	SELF-RIGHTEOUS

Great Gilly Hopkins Vocabulary

FEEBLE	ELABORATELY	EXPANSE	FANATIC	DIVERTED
HEFTING	SALVAGE	PSYCHOLOGISTS	LEERING	EMPHATICALLY
SEETHED	EMBRACE	FREE SPACE	CHANDELIER	DELINQUENCY
MONOGRAMMED	AUDIBLE	FLUTED	BELLIGERENTLY	OBLIGINGLY
VENGEANCE	KALEIDOSCOPIC	DELECTABLE	CULINARY	BARRACUDA

Great Gilly Hopkins Vocabulary

SEETHED	APPARITION	OBSCENITY	FRACAS	APPALLING
ANOINTED	GAUDIEST	FANATIC	ENGRAVED	LABORIOUSLY
VENGEANCE	RIFFLED	FREE SPACE	BELLIGERENTLY	ANONYMOUS
IMBECILE	SELF-RIGHTEOUS	INEXORABLY	FLUTED	DELINQUENCY
ENTHRALLED	LADEN	CONFIRMED	PIOUSLY	EMPHATICALLY

Great Gilly Hopkins Vocabulary

QUAVERING	AGONY	KALEIDOSCOPIC	EMBRACE	TENTATIVELY
WOEFULLY	OBLIGINGLY	FLIRTATION	DIVERTED	LEERING
BARRACUDA	CULINARY	FREE SPACE	SALVAGE	REPERTORY
SUBMISSION	CANOPIED	DELECTABLE	VARIATIONS	STRICKEN
MONOGRAMMED	ENGULFED	HEFTING	AUDIBLE	BENIGNLY

Great Gilly Hopkins Vocabulary

IRRITABILITY	KALEIDOSCOPIC	RIFFLED	BELLIGERENTLY	APPARITION
DELECTABLE	FEEBLE	SELF-RIGHTEOUS	INCOMPETENCE	CULINARY
GAUDIEST	DELINQUENCY	FREE SPACE	CHANDELIER	LABORIOUSLY
OBLIGINGLY	HEFTING	CANOPIED	LEERING	IMBECILE
TRIFLED	ENGULFED	FANATIC	EMPHATICALLY	AGONY

Great Gilly Hopkins Vocabulary

VARIATIONS	PSYCHOLOGISTS	ENGRAVED	TENTATIVELY	LADEN
EMBRACE	STRICKEN	OBSCENITY	PIOUSLY	REPERTORY
EXPANSE	SALVAGE	FREE SPACE	FLUTED	SEETHED
INEXORABLY	RELENTLESSLY	BENIGNLY	DIVERTED	BARRACUDA
EMBROIDERED	WOEFULLY	APPALLING	CONFIRMED	PERPETUAL

Great Gilly Hopkins Vocabulary

TENTATIVELY	OBLIGINGLY	FRACAS	DELECTABLE	OBSCENITY
EMBRACE	LEERING	DELINQUENCY	FLIRTATION	ANOINTED
STRICKEN	FUTILE	FREE SPACE	KALEIDOSCOPIC	FLUTED
INEXORABLY	HEFTING	MONOGRAMMED	SEETHED	APPARITION
BARRACUDA	GAUDIEST	LABORIOUSLY	EXPANSE	LADEN

Great Gilly Hopkins Vocabulary

VARIATIONS	FANATIC	INCOMPETENCE	REPERTORY	ENGRAVED
IMBECILE	ENTHRALLED	EMBROIDERED	WOEFULLY	ANONYMOUS
SUBMISSION	APPALLING	FREE SPACE	PERPETUAL	VENGEANCE
ELABORATELY	ENGULFED	SELF-RIGHTEOUS	PSYCHOLOGISTS	AUDIBLE
CHANDELIER	RIFFLED	TRIFLED	CULINARY	AGONY

Great Gilly Hopkins Vocabulary

ANOINTED	WOEFULLY	GAUDIEST	FUTILE	ELABORATELY
PSYCHOLOGISTS	CULINARY	ANONYMOUS	SELF-RIGHTEOUS	BELLIGERENTLY
RELENTLESSLY	IMBECILE	FREE SPACE	KALEIDOSCOPIC	VARIATIONS
OBLIGINGLY	ENTHRALLED	INCOMPETENCE	BARRACUDA	PIOUSLY
VENGEANCE	LABORIOUSLY	AGONY	BENIGNLY	DIVERTED

Great Gilly Hopkins Vocabulary

LADEN	REPERTORY	EXPANSE	INEXORABLY	SEETHED
EMPHATICALLY	FLUTED	TENTATIVELY	LEERING	ENGULFED
IRRITABILITY	FLIRTATION	FREE SPACE	QUAVERING	RIFFLED
OBSCENITY	DELECTABLE	HEFTING	SUBMISSION	CANOPIED
FEEBLE	FRACAS	APPARITION	EMBROIDERED	STRICKEN

Great Gilly Hopkins Vocabulary

FLIRTATION	LABORIOUSLY	PERPETUAL	AGONY	MONOGRAMMED
CANOPIED	CONFIRMED	LEERING	FEEBLE	EXPANSE
FLUTED	BENIGNLY	FREE SPACE	DIVERTED	PSYCHOLOGISTS
APPALLING	LADEN	FRACAS	DELECTABLE	RIFFLED
DELINQUENCY	SEETHED	PIOUSLY	WOEFULLY	SUBMISSION

Great Gilly Hopkins Vocabulary

FANATIC	HEFTING	INEXORABLY	ANOINTED	STRICKEN
VENGEANCE	RELENTLESSLY	BELLIGERENTLY	CULINARY	OBSCENITY
REPERTORY	SALVAGE	FREE SPACE	TENTATIVELY	EMPHATICALLY
GAUDIEST	ELABORATELY	ANONYMOUS	ENGULFED	SELF-RIGHTEOUS
EMBROIDERED	VARIATIONS	TRIFLED	FUTILE	OBLIGINGLY

Great Gilly Hopkins Vocabulary

OBSCENITY	INCOMPETENCE	ANOINTED	SEETHED	FANATIC
KALEIDOSCOPIC	DIVERTED	ENGULFED	GAUDIEST	RIFFLED
INEXORABLY	CULINARY	FREE SPACE	FLIRTATION	PIOUSLY
BENIGNLY	ENTHRALLED	RELENTLESSLY	MONOGRAMMED	PSYCHOLOGISTS
CONFIRMED	FUTILE	PERPETUAL	SUBMISSION	IRRITABILITY

Great Gilly Hopkins Vocabulary

SELF-RIGHTEOUS	ANONYMOUS	FRACAS	AGONY	DELINQUENCY
EMBROIDERED	STRICKEN	SALVAGE	LADEN	TENTATIVELY
DELECTABLE	AUDIBLE	FREE SPACE	ELABORATELY	WOEFULLY
EMBRACE	FEEBLE	CHANDELIER	EMPHATICALLY	EXPANSE
VENGEANCE	REPERTORY	FLUTED	VARIATIONS	APPALLING

Great Gilly Hopkins Vocabulary

FLIRTATION	SUBMISSION	FANATIC	ENGRAVED	SALVAGE
DELINQUENCY	ENGULFED	IMBECILE	BELLIGERENTLY	APPARITION
INEXORABLY	ANOINTED	FREE SPACE	FRACAS	QUAVERING
EMPHATICALLY	EMBRACE	STRICKEN	PSYCHOLOGISTS	FLUTED
DELECTABLE	LABORIOUSLY	TRIFLED	FEEBLE	EXPANSE

Great Gilly Hopkins Vocabulary

CANOPIED	KALEIDOSCOPIC	CHANDELIER	APPALLING	TENTATIVELY
DIVERTED	PERPETUAL	CONFIRMED	AGONY	BENIGNLY
ENTHRALLED	RIFFLED	FREE SPACE	HEFTING	ANONYMOUS
LEERING	OBLIGINGLY	CULINARY	FUTILE	SEETHED
LADEN	AUDIBLE	EMBROIDERED	OBSCENITY	GAUDIEST

Great Gilly Hopkins Vocabulary

CANOPIED	MONOGRAMMED	VARIATIONS	EMBRACE	DELINQUENCY
WOEFULLY	IRRITABILITY	SELF-RIGHTEOUS	INCOMPETENCE	EMBROIDERED
EXPANSE	ELABORATELY	FREE SPACE	TENTATIVELY	OBSCENITY
ANONYMOUS	PIOUSLY	AUDIBLE	LEERING	OBLIGINGLY
BENIGNLY	SUBMISSION	FLUTED	TRIFLED	FUTILE

Great Gilly Hopkins Vocabulary

AGONY	FRACAS	ENTHRALLED	LABORIOUSLY	GAUDIEST
HEFTING	BELLIGERENTLY	CULINARY	RIFFLED	ENGULFED
INEXORABLY	CHANDELIER	FREE SPACE	SEETHED	SALVAGE
FANATIC	REPERTORY	FLIRTATION	ENGRAVED	DIVERTED
STRICKEN	EMPHATICALLY	FEEBLE	BARRACUDA	APPALLING

Great Gilly Hopkins Vocabulary

PIOUSLY	GAUDIEST	TENTATIVELY	VARIATIONS	AGONY
OBLIGINGLY	SEETHED	FANATIC	IMBECILE	LADEN
FRACAS	CANOPIED	FREE SPACE	MONOGRAMMED	INCOMPETENCE
APPARITION	REPERTORY	CHANDELIER	BENIGNLY	ENGULFED
SUBMISSION	BELLIGERENTLY	OBSCENITY	FEEBLE	QUAVERING

Great Gilly Hopkins Vocabulary

HEFTING	TRIFLED	APPALLING	SALVAGE	ANOINTED
DIVERTED	EMBROIDERED	EMBRACE	VENGEANCE	ENGRAVED
STRICKEN	DELINQUENCY	FREE SPACE	ENTHRALLED	FLIRTATION
RIFFLED	CONFIRMED	RELENTLESSLY	AUDIBLE	LABORIOUSLY
PSYCHOLOGISTS	CULINARY	ANONYMOUS	SELF-RIGHTEOUS	PERPETUAL

www.ingramcontent.com/pod-product-compliance
Lightning Source LLC
Chambersburg PA
CBHW081455070526
44586CB00019B/2361